POEMS OF GRATITUDE
AND HOPE

Edited by
James Crews

Storey Publishing

The mission of Storey Publishing is to serve our customers by publishing practical information that encourages personal independence in harmony with the environment.

Edited by Liz Bevilacqua
Art direction and book design by Alethea Morrison
Text production by Slavica A. Walzl
Illustrations by © Dinara Mirtalipova

Storey books are available at special discounts when purchased in bulk for premiums and sales promotions as well as for fund-raising or educational use. Special editions or book excerpts can also be created to specification. For details, please call 800-827-8673, or send an email to sales@storey.com.

Storey Publishing
210 MASS MoCA Way
North Adams, MA 01247
storey.com

Printed in the United States by LSC Communications
10 9 8 7 6 5 4 3

Library of Congress Cataloging-in-Publication Data on file

**Joy is the happiness
that doesn't depend on what happens.**
Brother David Steindl-Rast

**Only the creative mind can make use of hope.
Only a creative people can wield it.**
Jericho Brown

CONTENTS

ACKNOWLEDGMENTS

Deep gratitude to the many people who helped to make this book a reality: the team at Storey Publishing, for agreeing to take a chance on a book of poetry, especially Deborah Balmuth, Liz Bevilacqua, Alee Moncy, Jennifer Travis, and Melinda Slaving, as well as Lauren Moseley at Algonquin Books for publicity support; Katie Rubinstein for making the connection and her beautiful work; everyone at A Network for Grateful Living, especially Kristi Nelson and Saoirse McClory, for their support of poetry; Brother David Steindl-Rast for his teachings on gratefulness, which we need now more than ever; Ted Kooser, for his enduring friendship, inspiration, and example of kindness; the late, great David Clewell, whose exuberant spirit not only made me fall in love with poetry, but also led me to future mentors Ron Wallace and Jesse Lee Kercheval; all of the poets included here for their generosity in sharing their work; Ross Gay for writing a foreword that is both a blessing and a poem in and of itself; Naomi Shihab Nye, Maria Popova, and Elizabeth Berg for their support of writing that makes us all feel more human; Garland Richmond, Diana Whitney, Heather Newman, Heather Swan, and Michelle Wiegers for essential support; my students at SUNY-Albany and Eastern Oregon University for giving me hope and serving as first readers; my husband, Brad Peacock, and our Crews and Peacock families, for reminding me every day why I'm so grateful to be alive.

FOREWORD

I have been spending a lot of time lately thinking about wit-
ness, about how witness itself is a kind of poetics, or poesis,
which means *making*. By which I mean I have been wondering
about how we make the world in our witnessing of it. Or maybe I
have come to understand, to believe, *how* we witness makes our
world. This is why attending to what we love, what we are aston-
ished by, what flummoxes us with beauty, is such crucial work.
Such rigorous work. Likewise, studying how we care, and are
cared for, how we tend and are tended to, how we give and are
given, is such necessary work. It makes the world. Witnessing
how we are loved and how we love makes the world. Witness
and study, I should say. Witness as study, I think I mean.

Truth is, we are mostly too acquainted with the opposite,
with the wreckage. It commands our attention, and for good
reason. We have to survive it. But even if we need to understand
the wreckage to survive it, it needn't be the primary object of
our study. The survival need be. The reaching and the holding
need be. The *here, have this* need be. The *come in, you can stay
here* need be. The *let's share it all* need be. The love need be.

The care need be. That which we are made by, held by, need be. Who's taken us in need be. Who's saved the seed need be. Who's planted the milkweed need be. Who's saved the water need be. Who's saved the forest need be. The forest need be. The water. The breathable air. That which witnessed us forth need be. How we have been loved need be. How we are loved need be.

How we need need be, too. Our radiant need. Our luminous and mycelial need. Our need immense and immeasurable. Our need absolute need be. And that study, that practice, that witness, is called gratitude. Our gratitude need be.

This is what I want to study. This is with whom.

Ross Gay

THE NECESSITY OF JOY

One day a few weeks ago, I woke up in a terrible mood. I've always been a morning person, relishing those early hours when the world is still asleep, before emails, texts, and the rest of my distractions take over. I love the ritual of making pour-over coffee for my husband and myself, inhaling the fragrant steam that curls up from the grounds as I pour on the boiling water. Yet this day, I couldn't shake my annoyance as I smashed a pat of cold, hard butter onto my toast, tearing a hole in the bread. I shook my head and scowled, then looked over at my husband who smiled. "What?" I said. He just stared deeply into my eyes and asked, "Are you happy to be alive today?" I glared at him at first, but I also let his question stop my mind. And in that gap, a rush of gratitude swept in. Yes, I was happy to be alive, happy to be standing in the kitchen next to the man I love, about to begin another day together. Happy to have coffee, food, and a warm place to live. Happy even to feel that dark mood swirling through me because it was also evidence of my aliveness.

Are you happy to be alive? The poems gathered in this book each ask, in their own ways, that same question, which has more relevance now than ever. As Brother David Steindl-Rast, the founder of A Network for Grateful Living, has famously pointed out: "In daily life, we must see that it is not happiness that makes us grateful. It is gratefulness that makes us happy." Paying attention to our lives is the first step toward gratitude and hope, and the poems in *How to Love the World* model for us the kind of mindfulness that is the gateway to a fuller, more sustainable happiness that can be called joy. Whether blessing a lawn full of common dandelions, or reminding us, as Tony Hoagland does, to "sit out in the sun and listen," these poets know that hope, no matter how slight it might seem, is as pressing a human need right now as food, water, shelter, or rest. We may survive without it, but we cannot thrive.

During these uncertain and trying times, we tell ourselves that joy is an indulgence we can no longer afford. And we've become all too familiar with the despair filling the airwaves and crowding our social media feeds, leading to what psychologists now call empathy or compassion fatigue, whereby we grow numb and disconnected from the suffering of others. We want to stay informed about what's going on in the world, yet we also know that absorbing so much negativity leaves us drained and hopeless. We know it's robbing us of the ability to be present to our own experience and grateful for something as simple as the moon, which is here, as Lahab Assef Al-Jundi points out, "to illuminate our illusion" of separateness from one another.

For many years, reading and writing poetry has been my personal source of delight, an antidote to the depression that can spring up out of nowhere. I now carve out what I call "soul time" for myself each day, making space for silence and reflection, even if it is just five or ten minutes, even if I have to wake up a little earlier to do it. The time I take to pause and read a favorite poem from a book, or jot down some small kindness from the day before, can utterly transform my mindset for the rest of the day. I invite you to use each poem in *How to Love the World* in a similar way, to make reading (and writing, if you wish) part of your own daily gratitude practice. Throughout the collection, I've also included reflective pauses, with specific suggestions for writing practices based upon the poems. When you encounter one of these, you may simply read that poem and reflection, then move on. Or you might keep a notebook nearby and stop to write, letting the guiding questions lead you more deeply into your own encounters with gratitude, hope, and joy. I encourage you to use any of these poems that spark something as jumping-off points for a journal entry, story, or poem of your own.

I trust in the necessity and pleasure of all kinds of creativity—from cooking a meal to fixing a car to sketching in the margins of a grocery list—but poetry is an art form especially suited to our challenging times. It helps us dive beneath the surface of our lives, and enter a place of wider, wilder, more universal knowing. And because poetry is made of the everyday material of language, we each have access to its ability to hold truths that normal conversation simply can't contain. When you find a poem that speaks to exactly what you've felt but had no way to name, a light bulb flashes in some hidden part of the self that you might have forgotten was there. I'll never forget the first time I read Ellen Bass's poem, "Any Common Desolation," and rushed to share it with my friends and family. "You may have to break your heart," Bass writes, suggesting that we might need to be more open and vulnerable to the world than we feel we can stand at times, but then she reminds us, "it isn't nothing to know even one moment alive." We need poems like the ones gathered here to ground us in our lives, to find in each new moment what Rosemerry Wahtola Trommer describes as, "the chance for joy, whole orchards of amazement."

James Crews, July 2020

Rosemerry Wahtola Trommer

HOPE

Hope has holes
in its pockets.
It leaves little
crumb trails
so that we,
when anxious,
can follow it.
Hope's secret:
it doesn't know
the destination—
it knows only
that all roads
begin with one
foot in front
of the other.

Ted Kooser

DANDELION

The first of a year's abundance of dandelions
is this single kernel of bright yellow
dropped on our path by the sun, sensing
that we might need some marker to help us
find our way through life, to find a path
over the snow-flattened grass that was
blade by blade unbending into green,
on a morning early in April, this happening
just at the moment I thought we were lost
and I'd stopped to look around, hoping
to see something I recognized. And there
it was, a commonplace dandelion, right
at my feet, the first to bloom, especially
yellow, as if pleased to have been the one,
chosen from all the others, to show us the way.

Barbara Crooker

PROMISE

This day is an open road
stretching out before you.
Roll down the windows.
Step into your life, as if it were a fast car.
Even in industrial parks,
trees are covered with white blossoms,
festive as brides, and the air is soft
as a well-washed shirt on your arms.
The grass has turned implausibly green.
Tomorrow, the world will begin again,
another fresh start. The blue sky stretches,
shakes out its tent of light. Even dandelions glitter
in the lawn, a handful of golden change.

AT THE AGE OF 18—ODE TO GIRLS OF COLOR

At the age of 5
I saw how we always pick the flower swelling with
    the most color.
The color distinguishes it from the rest, and tells us:
This flower should not be left behind.
But this does not happen in the case of colored girls.
Our color makes hands pull back, and we, left to grow
    alone,
stretching our petals to a dry sun.
At the age of 12
I blinked in the majesty of the color within myself,
blinded by the knowledge that a skinny black girl, a
    young brown teen,
has the power to light Los Angeles all night,
the radiance to heal all the scars left on this city's
    pavement.
Why had this realization taken so long,
when color pulses in all that is beauty and painting and
    human?
You see, long ago, they told me
that snakes and spiders have spots and vibrant bodies if
    they are poisonous.
In other words, being of color meant danger, warning,
    'do not touch'.
At the age of 18

I know my color is not warning, but a welcome.
A girl of color is a lighthouse, an ultraviolet ray of power,
    potential, and promise
My color does not mean caution, it means courage
my dark does not mean danger, it means daring,
my brown does not mean broken, it means bold backbone
    from working
twice as hard to get half as far.
Being a girl of color means I am key, path, and wonder all
    in one body.
At the age of 18
I am experiencing how black and brown can glow.
And glow I will, glow we will, vibrantly, colorfully;
not as a warning, but as promise,
that we will set the sky alight with our magic.

Dorianne Laux

IN ANY EVENT

If we are fractured
we are fractured
like stars
bred to shine
in every direction,
through any dimension,
billions of years
since and hence.

I shall not lament
the human, not yet.
There is something
more to come, our hearts
a gold mine
not yet plumbed,
an uncharted sea.

Nothing is gone forever.
If we came from dust
and will return to dust
then we can find our way
into anything.

What we are capable of
is not yet known,
and I praise us now,
in advance.

Laura Grace Weldon

ASTRAL CHORUS

Stars resonate like a huge musical instrument.
—*Bill Chaplin, asteroseismologist*

Late for chores after dinner with friends,
I walk up the darkening path,
my mind knitting something warm
out of the evening's words.
The woods are more shadow
than trees, barn a hulking shape on its slope.
I breathe in autumn's leaf-worn air, aware
I am glad to be in this place, this life.
The chickens have come in
from their wanderings. Lined up
like a choir, they croon soft lullabies.
A flock of stars stirs a navy-blue sky.
I can't hear them, but I'm told they
sing of things we have yet to learn.

Garret Keizer

MY DAUGHTER'S SINGING

I will miss the sound of her singing
through the wall that separates
her bathroom from ours, in the morning
before school, how she would harmonize
with the bare-navel angst
of some screaming Ophelia on her stereo,
though she had always seemed a contented kid,
a grower of rare gourds, an aficionado
of salamanders, and a babysitter prized
for her playful, earnest care, her love
of children so pure she seemed to become
a little child whenever she took one by the hand,
entering heaven so handily.
But it reminded me, that singing,
of the soul depths we never know,
even in those we love more than our souls,
so mad we are to anticipate the future,
and already I am talking—
a year to go before she goes
to college, and listen to me talking—
in the past tense as she sings.

David Romtvedt

SURPRISE BREAKFAST

One winter morning I get up early
to clean the ash from the grate
and find my daughter, eight, in the kitchen
thumping around pretending she has a peg leg

while also breaking eggs into a bowl—
separating yolks and whites, mixing oil
and milk. Her hands are smooth,
not from lack of labor but youth.

She's making pancakes for me, a surprise
I have accidentally ruined. "You never
get up early," she says, measuring
the baking powder, beating the egg whites.

It's true. When I wake, I roll to the side
and pull the covers over my head.
"It was too cold to sleep," I say.
"I thought I'd get the kitchen warm."

Aside from the scraping of the small flat shovel
on the iron grate, and the wooden spoon turning
in the bowl, the room is quiet. I lift the gray ash
and lay it carefully into a bucket to take outside.

"How'd you lose your leg?" I ask.
"At sea. I fell overboard in a storm
and a shark attacked me, but I'm fine."
She spins, a little batter flying from the spoon.

I can hear the popping of the oil in the pan.
"Are you ready?" she asks, thumping to the stove.
Fork in hand, I sit down, hoping that yes,
I am ready, or nearly so, or one day will be.

Ron Wallace

THE FACTS OF LIFE

She wonders how people get babies.
Suddenly vague and distracted,
we talk about "making love."
She's six and unsatisfied, finds
our limp answers unpersuasive.
Embarrassed, we stiffen, and try again,
this time exposing the stark naked words:
penis, vagina, sperm, womb, and egg.
She thinks we're pulling her leg.
We decide that it's time
to get passionate and insist.
But she's angry, disgusted.
Why do we always make fun of her?
Why do we lie?
We sigh, try cabbages, storks.
She smiles. That's more like it.
We talk on into the night, trying
magic seeds, good fairies, God . . .

FIFTEEN YEARS LATER, I SEE HOW IT WENT

They say you fall in love with your child
the moment you first hold them,
still covered in blood and vernix.
I held the strange being
just arrived from the womb and felt curious,
astonished, humble, nervous.
But love didn't come till later.
Came from holding him
while he was screaming. Waking with him
when I wanted to sleep. Bouncing him
when I wanted to be still. Love grew
as my ideas of myself diminished. Love grew
as he came into himself. Love grew
as I learned to let go of what I'd been told
and to trust the emerging form,
falling in love with the flawed beings we are.
Until I couldn't imagine being without him.
Until I was the one being born.

Kathryn Hunt

THE NEWBORNS

All through the night,
all through the long witless hallways of my sleep,
from my hospital bed I heard
the newborn babies cry, bewildered,
between worlds, like new arrivals anywhere,
unacquainted with the names of things.

That afternoon a kind nurse named Laura
had taken me for a stroll to exercise
the red line of my wound.
We stopped by the nursery window
and a flannel-swathed boy in a clear plastic cradle
was pushed to the glass. We peered at him
and said, "Welcome. You've come to Earth."
We laughed and shook our heads.

All through the night, all through the
drug-spangled rapture of my dreams,
I heard the newborn babies sing,
first one, then another. The fierce
beginning of their lament, that bright hiss,
those soft octaves of wonder.

Christen Pagett

SHELLS

The curl of your ear,
A tiny pearl of a shell
That I kiss so gently
You can barely feel it,
Barely hear it.

That pink flushing hot
With sleep,
Nape of your neck damp,
As I tuck the blankets too tight.

Remember when you were three
And held one to your face?
Was it a cockle shell, a conch shell?
Some polished swirl of light.

Wet sand on cheek,
You listened.

Like I listen,
To make sure you are
Still breathing.
Watching for that
Tiny throb of life
Pressing at your throat.

Laure-Anne Bosselaar

BUS STOP

Stubborn sleet. Traffic stuck on Sixth.
We cram the shelter, soaked, strain
to see the bus, except for a man next to me,
dialing his cell-phone. He hunches,
pulls his parka's collar over it, talks slow and low:
"It's daddy, hon. You do? Me too. Ask mom
if I can come see you now. Oh, okay,
Sunday then. Bye. Me too baby. Me too."
He snaps the phone shut, cradles it to his cheek,
holds it there. Dusk stains the sleet, minutes
slush by. When we board the bus,
that phone is still pressed to his cheek.

HOODIE

A gray hoodie will not protect my son
from rain, from the New England cold.

I see the partial eclipse of his face
as his head sinks into the half-dark

and shades his eyes. Even in our
quiet suburb with its unlocked doors,

I fear for his safety—the darkest child
on our street in the empire of blocks.

Sometimes I don't know who he is anymore
traveling the back roads between boy and man.

He strides a deep stride, pounds a basketball
into wet pavement. Will he take his shot

or is he waiting for the open-mouthed
orange rim to take a chance on him? I sing

his name to the night, ask for safe passage
from this borrowed body into the next

and wonder who could mistake him
for anything but good.

Terri Kirby Erickson

ANGEL

I used to see them walking, a middle-aged
man and his grown son, both wearing brown
trousers and white shirts like boys in a club,
or guys who like to simplify. But anyone
could see the son would never be a man who
walked without a hand to hold, a voice telling
him what to do. So the father held his son's
hand and whispered whatever it was the boy
needed to know, in tones so soft and low it
might have been the sound of wings pressing
together again and again. Maybe it was that
sound, since the father had the look of an angel
about him, or what we imagine angels should
be—a bit solemn-faced, with eyes that view
the world through a lens of kindness—who
sees every man's son as beautiful and whole.

Todd Davis

THANKFUL FOR NOW

Walking the river back home at the end
of May, locust in bloom, an oriole flitting
through dusky crowns, and the early night sky
going peach, day's late glow the color of that fruit's
flesh, dribbling down over everything, christening
my sons, the two of them walking before me
after a day of fishing, one of them placing a hand
on the other's shoulder, pointing toward a planet
that's just appeared, or the swift movement
of that yellow and black bird disappearing
into the growing dark, and now the light, pink
as a crabapple's flower, and my legs tired
from wading the higher water, and the rocks
that keep turning over, nearly spilling me
into the river, but still thankful for now
when I have enough strength to stay
a few yards behind them, loving this time
of day that shows me the breadth
of their backs, their lean, strong legs
striding, how we all go on in this cold water,
heading home to the sound of the last few
trout splashing, as mayflies float
through the shadowed riffles.

The Joy of Presence

In "Thankful for Now," we see Todd Davis pausing to appreciate an early evening scene while "walking the river back home" with his two sons. It is one thing to notice and beautifully describe the elements of nature, as Davis does— "the early night sky going peach, day's late glow the color of that fruit's flesh"—but it is another to cultivate the kind of presence that can make us all "thankful for now," no matter our particular circumstances. As Eckhart Tolle has written: "You don't have to wait for something 'meaningful' to come into your life so that you can finally enjoy what you do. There is more meaning in joy than you will ever need."

We often strive to reach for experiences and things beyond what we have in this moment and forget the power of pausing and making space to say thank you for what's right in front of us. Writing of his sons, Davis finds gratitude in simply noticing "the breadth of their backs, their lean, strong legs striding."

Invitation for Writing and Reflection

When was the last time you felt yourself simply "thankful for now," for the present moment that allowed you to notice and appreciate every detail of life as it was just then?

Barbara Crooker

AUTISM POEM: THE GRID

A black and yellow spider hangs motionless in its web,
and my son, who is eleven and doesn't talk, sits
on a patch of grass by the perennial border, watching.
What does he see in his world, where geometry
is more beautiful than a human face?
Given chalk, he draws shapes on the driveway:
pentagons, hexagons, rectangles, squares.
The spider's web is a grid,
transecting the garden in equal parts.

Sometimes he stares through the mesh on a screen.
He loves things that are perforated:
toilet paper, graham crackers, coupons
in magazines, loves the order of the tiny holes,
the way the boundaries are defined. And real life
is messy and vague. He shrinks back to a stare,
switches off his hearing. And my heart,
not cleanly cut like a valentine, but irregular
and many-chambered, expands and contracts,
contracts and expands.

Diana Whitney

KINDERGARTEN STUDIES
THE HUMAN HEART

Nothing like a valentine,
pink construction paper
glue-sticked to doilies downstairs
in preschool, the sand table
filled with flour, the Fours
driving trucks through silky powder,
white clouds rising
to dust their round cheeks.
Up here, the Fives are all business:
four chambers on the chalkboard,
four rooms colored hard
in thick-tipped marker, red and red,
blue and blue, oxygen rich
and oxygen poor, the branching vine
of the aorta hanging
its muscled fruit, carmine
blood-flower blooming
in a thick jungle.
My girl squeezes her fist
to show me the size of it.
Pulses it like a live animal.
Taps the double rhythm
that never stops, not a trot
but the echo of a trot, not a drum

but the echo of a drum,
small palms on the art table
laying down the backbeat:
become become become.

Gail Newman

VALENTINE'S DAY

Now that my father is gone,
I send my mother flowers.

She sleeps under a blue blanket
alone on her side of the bed,
fluffing both pillows just so.

She balances as she walks,
one hand skimming the wall.
Sometimes she doesn't know
where her friends are, who is still living.

Einstein was right about time
moving in two directions at once,
how everything that happens
seems to have happened before,

how when I stand before the mirror
combing my hair, I see my mother's eyes,
and happiness wells up like a wave
without warning.

My mother looks forward
to a lunch of bread and cheese,
a glass of apple juice.

She speaks of the weather,
today being only itself.
Her time is reeling in, a line cast
from shore. But how she loves
the sea, the horizon, the flaming sun!

My mother, who knows the brutal world,
who survived while others did not,
says, *Me? I had it easy.*

Abigail Carroll

IN GRATITUDE

For *h*, tiny fire
    in the hollow of the throat,
        opener of every *hey,*

hi, how are you?,
    hello; chums with *c,*
        with *t,* shy lover of *s;*

there and not
    there—never seen,
        hardly heard, yet

real as air
    fluttering the oak,
        holding up the hawk;

the sound
    of a yawn, of sleep, of heat,
        a match, its quivering

orange flame
    turning wood into light,
        light into breath;

the sound
    of stars if stars
        could be heard, perhaps

the sound
    of space; life speaking life:
        warm air endowed

to hard clay—
    a heart, hurt,
        a desire to be healed—

the work
    of bees stuck in the nubs
        of hollyhocks

and columbine, time
    to the extent that time
        is light, is bright

as the match,
    the flame of the sun,
        real as the muffled hush

of sleep,
    the fluttering oak,
        a moth, the silent *oh*

in the throat
    when a hand is laid
        upon the shoulder;

hunger—
    the body's empty cry
        for filling, for loving,

for knowing
    the intimacy of breath,
        of half-breathed words

fragile as the stars:
    hollow, hush,
        holy.

Michelle Wiegers

HELD OPEN

After the band concert, we filed out
of the high school auditorium
where the door seemingly stood open
all by itself. As I stepped into the hallway,
there stood one student's grandmother,
smiling as she held the door
for the crowd, her eyes searching
for the grandson she wanted to hug.

The embrace of this night of music
still wrapped its warm arms around me,
as if I'd just been held for over an hour
by the deep tones of the bari sax,
the stunning runs of the flutes, which caught
my breath, my son's steady rhythms
still pulsing in my chest,
as I stepped out into the night air.

David Graham

LISTENING FOR YOUR NAME

As a father steals into his child's half-lit bedroom
slowly, quietly, standing long and long
counting the breaths before finally slipping
back out, taking care not to wake her,

and as that night-lit child is fully awake the whole
time, with closed eyes, measured breathing,
savoring a delicious blessing she couldn't
name but will remember her whole life,

how often we feel we're being watched over,
or that we're secretly looking in on the ones
we love, even when they are far away,
or even as they are lost in the sleep

no one wakes from—what we know
and what we feel can fully coincide, like love
and worry, like taking care in full silence
and secrecy, like darkness and light together.

Heather Swan

ANOTHER DAY FILLED WITH
SLEEVES OF LIGHT,

and I carry ripened plums,
waiting to find the one
who is interested in tasting.

How can we ever be known?

Today the lily sends up
a fifth white-tipped tendril, the promise
of another flower opening,
and I think, this must mean this plant
is happy, here, in this house, by this window.
Is this the right deduction?

The taller plant leans and leans toward the light.
I turn it away, and soon its big hands are reaching again
toward what nourishes it,
but which it can never touch.

Couldn't the yellowing leaves of the maple
and their falling also be a sign of joy?
Another kind of leaning into.
A letting go of one thing
to fall into another.
A kind of trust I cannot imagine.

Annie Lighthart

A CURE AGAINST POISONOUS THOUGHT

Believe the world goes on
and this bee bending
in honeysuckle just one
of a mighty nation, golden
beads thrumming
a long invisible thread.

In the green drift of an afternoon,
the body is not root but wick:
the press of light surrounds it.

Mary McCue

FORGIVENESS

How does it creep into arteries,
level blood pressure
and wipe clean
the slate of anger
held close to the chest?

Look long into the mirror,
be tender with the face you see,
then to the blistered past,
the entire landscape,
the smallest detail
as in a Brueghel painting,

then revise and revise
until the story changes shape
and you, no longer the jailor,
have learned to love
what is left.

Heather Lanier

TWO WEEKS AFTER A SILENT RETREAT

How quickly I lose my love
of all things. I nearly flick an ant
off the cliff of an armchair.

But remember, Self,
the week you spent
enveloped in psalms

intoned by monks?
By Wednesday you beheld

a three-balled body
creeping around
the onionskin of your book,

its six teensy toothpick legs
bent into all manner of
delicate angles.

Your chest became
a doorway
to a spacious unmarked

heaven. You loved the ant.
The kingdom,
said Christ,

is at hand, meaning
not ticking above

in a time bomb of gold-
paved streets
but tapping its antennae

along the heart line
of your imperfect palm.

The Kingdom at Hand

Stepping outside of life, even for a short while, can help us return with a new perspective on what seemed unworkable before. Though such a wide-open embrace of life never lasts forever, it can be enough to know that it waits within us, accessible when we need it the most. Heather Lanier illustrates this in her poem, as she remembers her own time of reflection while on retreat, when her "chest became a doorway to a spacious unmarked heaven." Such moments often appear after periods of stillness, whether on an actual retreat, at church, or while spending the day outdoors, away from our screens.

Yet our lives do not unfold as a single, unbroken stretch of gratefulness and hope. We are humans living in an imperfectly human world, after all, and so we easily lose our reverence and "love of all things" in the midst of busyness, worry, and strife. We fall out of the practice of patience. But as Lanier points out, we can remind ourselves that the gate to the kingdom at hand remains open anytime we choose to pass through, and the reward for close attention to our lives, even if it is simply to save the life of an ant, is the heaven of a fuller presence in the here and now.

Invitation for Writing and Reflection

Think back to a time when you brought yourself back to the moment at hand and found the world vivid and lovable again. You might begin with Lanier's first line, "How quickly I lose my love," and see where that leads you.

Jane Hirshfield

TODAY, WHEN I COULD DO NOTHING

Today, when I could do nothing,
I saved an ant.

It must have come in with the morning paper,
still being delivered
to those who shelter in place.

A morning paper is still an essential service.

I am not an essential service.

I have coffee and books,
time,
a garden,
silence enough to fill cisterns.

It must have first walked
the morning paper, as if loosened ink
taking the shape of an ant.

Then across the laptop computer—warm—
then onto the back of a cushion.

Small black ant, alone,
crossing a navy cushion,
moving steadily because that is what it could do.

Set outside in the sun,
it could not have found again its nest.
What then did I save?

It did not move as if it was frightened,
even while walking my hand,
which moved it through swiftness and air.

Ant, alone, without companions,
whose ant-heart I could not fathom—
how is your life, I wanted to ask.

I lifted it, took it outside.

This first day when I could do nothing,
contribute nothing
beyond staying distant from my own kind,
I did this.

Laura Ann Reed

RED THYME

In the red thyme
that crawls
languidly
between stepping stones
time stops
as bees
thrust their passion
deep into the promise
of tiny crimson-purple
blooms.

Where blossom
ends
and bee
begins

are the first words
of a lullaby
the world sings
while it rocks you
as you fall
awake
in the later years
of a life
spent mostly
sound
asleep.

Laura Foley

THE ONCE INVISIBLE GARDEN

How did I come to be
this particular version of me,
and not some other, this morning
of purple delphiniums blooming,
like royalty—destined
to meet these three dogs
asleep at my feet, and not others—
this soft summer morning,
sitting on her screened porch
become ours, our wind chime,
singing of wind and time,
yellow-white digitalis
feeding bees and filling me—
and more abundance to come:
basil, tomatoes, zucchini.
What luck or fate, instinct,
or grace brought me here?—
in shade, beneath hidden stars,
a soft, summer morning,
seeing with my whole being,
love made visible.

James Crews

DOWN TO EARTH

The heart of a farmer
is made of muscle
and clay that aches
for return to earth.
And when the sky
releases a steady rain,
massaging each row
of sprouted beans,
my husband leans out
of the car window
and opens his hand
to hold that water
for a single instant,
his heart now beating
in sync with rain
seeping through layers
to kiss the roots
of every plant alive
on this living, breathing
planet on whose back
we were granted
permission to live
for a limited time.

Freya Manfred

OLD FRIENDS

Old friends are a steady spring rain,
or late summer sunshine edging into fall,
or frosted leaves along a snowy path—
a voice for all seasons saying, I know you.
The older I grow, the more I fear I'll lose my old friends,
as if too many years have scrolled by
since the day we sprang forth, seeking each other.

Old friend, I knew you before we met.
I saw you at the window of my soul—
I heard you in the steady millstone of my heart
grinding grain for our daily bread.
You are sedimentary, rock-solid cousin earth,
where I stand firmly, astonished by your grace and truth.
And gratitude comes to me and says:

"Tell me anything and I will listen.
Ask me anything, and I will answer you."

Brad Peacock

LET IT RAIN

I'm not sure why I did my best to outrun you.
Perhaps I had forgotten how your touch
makes me feel alive, like the gentle hands
of my husband reaching out to console me.
I smile, feeling the first drops from the sky
igniting my senses, calling forth the little boy inside
who wants more, to feel it pour. This is not
a shower that will extinguish the light
I've found within. It is a rain that will soak me through,
down to bone, baptizing me again and again,
as I walk these gravel roads that have helped me heal.
Droplets now fall from the brim of my hat,
streaming down my cheeks like the time I cried out,
begging for the shame to subside, wondering
if I had the strength to live this life anymore.

Molly Fisk

AGAINST PANIC

You recall those times, I know you do, when the sun
lifted its weight over a small rise to warm your face,
when a parched day finally broke open, real rain
sluicing down the sidewalk, rattling city maples
and you so sure the end was here, life a house of cards
tipped over, falling, hope's last breath extinguished
in a bitter wind. Oh, friend, search your memory again—
beauty and relief are still there, only sleeping.

Naomi Shihab Nye

OVER THE WEATHER

We forget about the spaciousness
above the clouds

but it's up there. The sun's up there too.

When words we hear don't fit the day,
when we worry
what we did or didn't do,
what if we close our eyes,
say any word we love
that makes us feel calm,
slip it into the atmosphere
and rise?

Creamy miles of quiet.
Giant swoop of blue.

Paula Gordon Lepp

NOTIONS

Look at the silver lining, they say.
But what if, instead,
I pluck it off
and use that tensile strand to bind
myself to those things I do not
want to lose sight of.

Families knit together by evening walks,
board games, laughter.
The filament fixing us to friends
no matter the distance apart.
A braid of gratitude for small kindnesses.
The thin gauge wire of loss.

Let me twist that lining
around my finger,
it's silvery glint a reminder
of just how quickly life can change.
I will remember to love more.
I will remember to give more.

I will remember to be still.

I will knot the string tightly.
So it won't slip away.
So I won't forget.

Ellen Bass

ANY COMMON DESOLATION

can be enough to make you look up
at the yellowed leaves of the apple tree, the few
that survived the rains and frost, shot
with late afternoon sun. They glow a deep
orange-gold against a blue so sheer, a single bird
would rip it like silk. You may have to break
your heart, but it isn't nothing
to know even one moment alive. The sound
of an oar in an oarlock or a ruminant
animal tearing grass. The smell of grated ginger.
The ruby neon of the liquor store sign.
Warm socks. You remember your mother,
her precision a ceremony, as she gathered
the white cotton, slipped it over your toes,
drew up the heel, turned the cuff. A breath
can uncoil as you walk across your own muddy yard,
the big dipper pouring night down over you, and everything
you dread, all you can't bear, dissolves
and, like a needle slipped into your vein—
that sudden rush of the world.

Returning to the World

When the world seems incomprehensible and its ills too many, I often retreat to the natural world, looking up "at the yellowed leaves of the apple tree" to calm my mind and try to make sense of our sometimes violent, divided culture. "Any common desolation," as Ellen Bass says, can send us into a frenzy, can glue us to our screens; but it is more healing if we get outside of our minds and commune with "that sudden rush" of the actual world again.

It can be painful to be so open to the world ("You may have to break your heart"), but as Bass points out, it is more than worth it "to know even one moment alive." What truly lifts us back into the flow is noticing each small thing that sparks our senses, whether it be "the sound of an oar," "the smell of grated ginger," or simply "warm socks."

Invitation for Writing and Reflection
What seemingly small joys bring you back to that "sudden rush of the world" even in the midst of worry or fear? How does it feel when gratitude and hope reawaken the heart to what's around you?

LANGUAGE, PRAYER, AND GRACE

Language is no more than the impressions
left by birds nesting in snow.

Prayer is the path opened
by a leopard leaping through the brush.

And grace is how the water parts for a fish
letting it break surface.

Jane Hirshfield

THE FISH

There is a fish
that stitches
the inner water
and the outer water together.

Bastes them
with its gold body's flowing.

A heavy thread
follows that transparent river,
secures it—
the broad world we make daily,
daily give ourselves to.

Neither imagined
nor unimagined,
neither winged nor finned,
we walk the luminous seam.
Knot it.
Flow back into the open gills.

Patricia Fargnoli

REINCARNATE

I want to come back as that ordinary
garden snail, carting my brown-striped spiral shell
onto the mushroom which has sprouted
after overnight rain so I can stretch
my tentacles toward the slightly drooping
and pimpled raspberry, sweet and pulsing—
a thumb that bends on its stalk from the crown
of small leaves, weighed down by the almost
translucent shining drop of dew I have
been reaching and reaching toward my whole life.

Linda Hogan

INNOCENCE

There is nothing more innocent
than the still-unformed creature I find beneath soil,
neither of us knowing what it will become
in the abundance of the planet.
It makes a living only by remaining still
in its niche.
One day it may struggle out of its tender
pearl of blind skin
with a wing or with vision
leaving behind the transparent.

I cover it again, keep laboring,
hands in earth, myself a singular body.
Watching things grow,
wondering how
a cut blade of grass knows
how to turn sharp again at the end.

This same growing must be myself,
not aware yet of what I will become
in my own fullness
inside this simple flesh.

Farnaz Fatemi

EVERYTHING IS MADE OF LABOR

The inchworm's trajectory:
pulse of impulse. The worm
is tender. It won't live
long. Its green glows.
It found a place to go.
Arrange us with meaning,
the words plead. Find the thread
through the dark.

Susan Kelly-DeWitt

APPLE BLOSSOMS

One evening in winter
when nothing has been enough,
when the days are too short,

the nights too long
and cheerless, the secret
and docile buds of the apple

blossoms begin their quick
ascent to light. Night
after interminable night

the sugars pucker and swell
into green slips, green
silks. And just as you find

yourself at the end
of winter's long, cold
rope, the blossoms open

like pink thimbles
and that black dollop
of shine called

bumblebee stumbles in.

Nancy Miller Gomez

GROWING APPLES

There is big excitement in C block today.
On the window sill,
in a plastic ice cream cup
a little plant is growing.
This is all the men want to talk about:
how an apple seed germinated
in a crack of damp concrete;
how they tore open tea bags
to collect the leaves, leached them
in water, then laid the sprout onto the bed
made of Lipton. How this finger of spring
dug one delicate root down
into the dark fannings and now
two small sleeves of green
are pushing out from the emerging tip.
The men are tipsy with this miracle.
Each morning, one by one,
they go to the window and check
the progress of the struggling plant.
All through the day they return
to stand over the seedling
and whisper.

Danusha Laméris

ASPEN

They tower above the hilltop,
yellow leaves rustling the air
in a kind of muffled conversation.

And when a breeze bends
their upper branches
they tilt sideways
in the gesture of attentive listeners.

And so, we sit together in silence,
old friends who don't need to speak.

Though sometimes they murmur
amongst themselves,
the kind of banter that once
soothed me as a child
drifting off to sleep

while my parents carried on
upstairs, talking after dinner
with their guests.

Now, a red-winged blackbird
lands on a slender branch
and is lost among shuffling leaves.

Now, a cloud passes overhead—
my mother's silk scarf
trailing on the wind.

Is this what it is to be alone?
This being with my tall,
branched sisters?

Then let me sit
in their lengthening shadow
as the day wanes,
and the hours of my life wane,

and the evening starts to fall,
and the night comes
with its quiet company of stars.

Margaret Hasse

WITH TREES

for Norton Stillman

Something I've forgotten calls me away
from the picnic table to tall trees
at the far end of the clearing.
I remember lying on grass
being still, studying forks of branches
with their thousands of leaves.
While trees accrued their secret rings
life spread a great canopy
of family, work, ordinary activity.
I mislaid what once moved me.

Today I have time to follow
the melody of green wherever it goes,
a tune, maybe hummed
when I was too young
to have the words I wanted
and know how a body returns
to familiar refrains.

Now like a child, I sit down, lie back,
look up at the crowns of maple,
needled spruce and a big-hearted boxwood.
Fugitive birds dart in and out.
In the least little wind, birch leaves turn

and flash silver like a school of minnows.
Clouds range in the blue sky
above earth's great geniuses
of shelter and shade.

Kim Stafford

SHELTER IN PLACE

Long before the pandemic, the trees
knew how to guard one place with
roots and shade. Moss found
how to hug a stone for life.
Every stream works out how
to move in place, staying home
even as it flows generously
outward, sending bounty far.
Now is our time to practice—
singing from balconies, sending
words of comfort by any courier,
kindling our lonesome generosity
to shine in all directions like stars.

Heather Newman

MISSING KEY

The doors are locked and I'm searching for a way in.
I circle my house intent on finding a crack in the system
I painstakingly created, a loose bolt, a faulty window.
It's still light in Vermont but in one hour the sun will dip
behind the mountain, temperatures will fall, and I may still
be stuck outside, cursing. There are friends. There
    are neighbors.
Or I could resolve nothing, sit on the cool grass and wait.
On my iPhone, I view my furious attempts to break in
recorded on the outdoor cameras. There are family
    members
who hold a key, but rescues have never worked for me
    in the past.
I consider places for lost or hidden keys. They say
    gratitude is a key.
Solitude is a mountain. There are pines, cedars and
    hemlocks,
a range against the mango-magenta horizon,
a red-tailed hawk circling its prey.

Michael Kiesow Moore

CLIMBING THE GOLDEN MOUNTAIN

Silence is the golden mountain.

—*Jack Kerouac*

Listen. Turn
everything
off. When
the noise
of our lives
drifts away,
when the
chatter of
our minds
sinks into
that perfect
lake of nothing,
then, oh
then we can
apprehend
that golden
mountain,
always there,
waiting for
us to be
still enough
to hear it.

Laura Foley

TO SEE IT

We need to separate to see
the life we've made.
We need to leave our house
where someone waits for us, patiently,
warm beneath the sheets.
We need to don a sweater, a coat, mittens,
wrap a scarf around our neck,
stride down the road,
a cold winter morning,
and turn our head back,
to see it—perched
on the top of the hill, our life
lit from inside.

Jacqueline Jules

UNCLOUDED VISION

Her lenses, implanted
to uncloud aging eyes,
sparkle now like a bit
of glitter on a card,
rhinestones on a T-shirt.

Twinkle in her eye. An old cliché.
Common long before
surgery was routine, suggesting
joy or affection—intangibles
that lift heels off concrete,
make us notice yellow petals
pushing through sidewalk cracks.

My grandmother
now visits museums again,
marvels at details, stops to read
each acrylic label on the wall.

Danusha Laméris

IMPROVEMENT

The optometrist says my eyes
are getting better each year.
Soon he'll have to lower my prescription.
What's next? The light step I had at six?
All the gray hairs back to brown?
Skin taut as a drum?

My improved eyes and I
walked around town and celebrated.

We took in the letters
of the marquee, the individual leaves
filling out the branches of the sycamore,
an early moon.

So much goes downhill: joints
wearing out with every mile,
the delicate folds of the eardrum
exhausted from years of listening.
I'm grateful for small victories.

The way the heart still beats time
in the cathedral of the ribs.

And the mind, watching its parade
of thoughts, enter and leave,
begins to see them for what they are:
jugglers, fire swallowers, acrobats,
tossing their batons into the air.

Grateful for Small Victories

In "Improvement," Danusha Laméris recounts the rare experience of a part of her body actually getting better with age and invites us to celebrate the good news with her. "So much goes downhill," she says, reminding us of the body's fragility and vulnerability. Yet she also urges us to be "grateful for small victories," for the fact that the heart carries on "in the cathedral of the ribs," and that the endlessly busy mind keeps sending out its "parade of thoughts." I love the way the speaker of this poem seems to detach from her own anxieties and intrusive thoughts, even playfully seeing them as "jugglers, fire swallowers, acrobats" meant to entertain, and not to be obeyed. And in her question, "What's next?," I also hear the willingness to have hope that other things in her life, and in the world, might begin to improve as well.

Invitation for Writing and Reflection

Write your own celebration of your "small victories," things you managed to accomplish no matter how slight they might seem. Whatever your list, try to capture that same sense of gratitude and joy for things that went well for you.

Jack Ridl

AFTER SPENDING THE MORNING
BAKING BREAD

Our cat lies across the stove's front burners,
right leg hanging over the oven door. He
is looking into the pantry where his bowl
sits full on the counter. His smaller dish,
the one for his splash of cream, sits empty.
Say yes to wanting to be this cat. Say
yes to wanting to lie across the leftover
warmth, letting it rise into your soft belly,
spreading into every twitch of whisker, twist
of fur and cell, through the Mobius strip
of your bloodstream. You won't know
you will die. You won't know the mice
do not exist for you. If a lap is empty and
warm, you will land on it, feel an unsteady
hand along your back, fingers scratching
behind your ear. You will purr.

Wally Swist

RADIANCE

Over your gray and white oval marble-top kitchen table,
the meeting of our eyes makes the room grow brighter.
Our faces, layer after layer, become so vibrant

the light appears to crest in waves.
We have become changed by it, nothing can be
the same after it. When I bend down to touch

the shape of deer tracks in the damp sand, it is in
the same way I place my fingers over your body.
When I stand beside a freshet in a meadow

the sun catches the rings of the water's long ripples
in the wind, that is the same glimmer we hold
when our eyes meet in the kitchen over

your gray and white oval marble-top table.
Every day for the rest of my life, yours is the face
I want to see when I awake in the morning.

Kristen Case

MORNING

Against all probability our bulbs have blossomed,
opened their white rooms, given their assent.
I pull myself from your breathing to take a closer look.
It happened overnight.

Outside a flock of birds folds and unfolds its single body.
I start the coffee. Light comes
from impossible directions.

You are still asleep.
I cup the curve of your skull with my hand.
Alive, sleeping.
Light rises on the flame-colored bricks.

Ross Gay

WEDDING POEM

for Keith and Jen

Friends I am here to modestly report
seeing in an orchard
in my town
a goldfinch kissing
a sunflower
again and again
dangling upside down
by its tiny claws
steadying itself by snapping open
like an old-timey fan
its wings
again and again,
until, swooning, it tumbled off
and swooped back to the very same perch,
where the sunflower curled its giant
swirling of seeds
around the bird and leaned back
to admire the soft wind
nudging the bird's plumage,
and friends I could see
the points on the flower's stately crown
soften and curl inward
as it almost indiscernibly lifted

the food of its body
to the bird's nuzzling mouth
whose fervor
I could hear from
oh 20 or 30 feet away
and see from the tiny hulls
that sailed from their
good racket,
which good racket, I have to say
was making me blush,
and rock up on my tippy-toes,
and just barely purse my lips
with what I realize now
was being, simply, glad,
which such love,
if we let it,
makes us feel.

Jehanne Dubrow

PLEDGE

Now we are here at home, in the little nation
of our marriage, swearing allegiance to the table
we set for lunch or the windchime on the porch,
its easy dissonance. Even in our shared country,
the afternoon allots its golden lines
so that we're seated, both in shadow, on opposite
ends of a couch and two gray dogs between us.
There are acres of opinions in this house.
I make two cups of tea, two bowls of soup,
divide an apple equally. If I were a patriot,
I would call the blanket we spread across our bed
the only flag—some nights we've burned it
with our anger at each other. Some nights
we've welcomed the weight, a woolen scratch
on both our skins. My love, I am pledging
to this republic, for however long we stand,
I'll watch with you the rain's arrival in our yard.
We'll lift our faces, together, toward the glistening.

Angela Narciso Torres

AMORES PERROS

Sometimes I love you
the way my dog loves
his all-beef chew bone,
worrying the knuckled

corners from every angle,
mandibles working
like pistons. His eyes glaze
over with a faraway look

that says he won't quit
till he reaches the soft
marrow. His paws prop
the bone upright,

it slips—he can't clutch it
tight enough, bite hard
enough. A dog's paws
weren't meant for gripping.

And sometimes I love you
the way my dog brushes
his flank nonchalant
against my legs, then flops

on the floor beside me
while I read or watch TV.
His heft warms.
One of us is hungry,

the other needs
to pee. But we sit,
content as wildflowers.
Minutes pass. Hours.

Noah Davis

MENDING

Something there is that doesn't love a wall,
That wants it down.
—*Robert Frost*

When I lie down with your
back against my chest, I think of how
my grandfather stacked river stone,
one upon another, building a wall
along the edge of the meadow.
And as my palm holds your hip,
I imagine the ball of bone
beneath the flesh, resting
like the cat at the foot of the bed.
And just as my grandfather would walk
the walls in April to find where
stones had cracked and crumbled,
I meander your body, placing my lips
along the backs of your legs, the bend
in your back, your neck that strains
under the day's labor. And where lips
cannot reach, words act like the oval rocks
we wedged into crevices, saving the wall
that keeps the world from our bed.

Penny Harter

IN THE DARK

At bedtime, my grandson's breath
rasps in and out of fragile lungs.
Holding the nebulizer mask
over his nose and mouth,
I rock him on my lap and hum
a lullaby to comfort him.

The nebulizer hisses as steroids
stream into his struggling chest,
and suddenly he also starts to hum,
his infant voice rising and falling
on the same few notes—some hymn
he must have learned while in the womb
or carried here from where he was before—
a kind of plainsong, holy and hypnotic
in the dark.

Nathan Spoon

A CANDLE IN THE NIGHT

Stone is tender
to lichen.
Lichen is tender
to the earth and its other
inhabitants. What are
you and I tender to?

When a black hole
swallows a star,
it must do so
tenderly, since
a universe hinges
on tenderness.

At midnight
your candle burns
with tenderness,
dream-like in an amber
votive, its flame
flickering tenderly.

Francine Marie Tolf

PRAISE OF DARKNESS

We touch one another
with defter fingers
at night.

Rain sounds different,
its steady falling
a remembered wisdom.

What if the dark waters
waiting to carry us home
slept inside every one of us?

We were loved
before stars existed.
We are older than light.

Judith Chalmer

AN ESSAY ON AGE

It was a day to sing the praises of fire,
to bow to its purpose,

toes stretched apart, layers peeled,
our bodies gathered

into their warmest folds.
It was a day of mists, of freezing

and love. Now the night
when it returns will be kinder.

Now the moon will dominate
the dogs, sending them wild

into the burdock and we will have them
for hours on their backs.

This is the bright snap of apple, catch
in the throat—you realize how deeply

you have loved. You blow hard
on the flames and each day

is remembered mainly for the brush
of lips, for the way we stand

hip to hip in sheets of rain,
almost covered, enough.

Ted Kooser

EASTER MORNING

A misty rain pushed up against the windows
as if the house were flying through a cloud,
the drops too light, too filled with light to run,
suspended on the glass, each with the same
reflections: barn and yard and garden, grayed.

Then, suddenly appearing, burning in the quince
that soon will bloom, a cardinal, just one
milligram of red allotted to each droplet,
but each a little heavier for picking up
that splash of color, overfilled and spilling,
stumbling headlong down the chilly pane.

Andrea Potos

THE CARDINAL REMINDS ME

It sweeps and arcs across my path
almost every day on my walk to the café,
under sun or cloud, its red
seems lit from inside, a brightness
bold as the lipstick my mother wore
no matter the day or the time,
no matter how near to the end
she got, even two days before the last—
the young dark-haired nurse applying it
for her while I sat near, my own
lips trembling from fear or hope
I could not tell, I could not separate anything,
not now either—the bright flame of this bird
recalling me to loss, or to joy.

Marjorie Saiser

WHEN LIFE SEEMS A TO-DO LIST

When the squares of the week fill
with *musts* and *shoulds*,

when I swim in the heaviness of it,
the headlines, the fear and hate,

then with luck, something like a slice of moon
will arrive clean as a bone

and beside it on that dark slate
a star will lodge near the cusp

and with luck I will have you
to see it with, the two of us,

fools stepping out the backdoor
in our pajamas.

Is that Venus?—I think so—Let's
call it Venus, cuddling up to the moon

and there are stars further away
sending out rays that will not

reach us in our lifetimes
but we are choosing, before the chaos

starts up again,
to stand in this particular light.

Lahab Assef Al-Jundi

MOON

Companion of lonesome hearts.
Dreamy shepherd of starry-eyed lovers.
Cratered dusty-faced rock.

This night you shine through
is just a shadow.
Our smallness makes us believe
the whole universe is immersed in darkness.
Midday sun burns on the other side.
Daylight everywhere!

Moon,
perhaps you are here to illuminate
our illusion?

If all suns are extinguished,
all moons and planets collapsed
into black holes,
what tint would space be?
What are colors without eyes?
How do we sense a vibrating universe?

Go ahead and laugh, hanging moon,
I raise my cup to you—
patient teacher.

Crystal S. Gibbins

BECAUSE THE NIGHT YOU ASKED

for Josh
with first and last line by Linda Pastan

Because the night you asked me
the moon shone like a quarter
in the sky; because the leaves
were the color of wine at our feet;
because, like you, there was a private
sense of absence in my every day;
because in your arms my heart grows
plump as a finch; because we both
pause at the sight of heavy branches
burdened with fruit, the sound
of apples dropping to the ground;
because you hold no secrets;
because I knew what I wanted;
because we both love the snow,
the ice, the feeling of a long deadening
freeze and the mercy of a thaw;
because you gave me an empty
beach on a warm day in fall,
and a feeling that we might stay
for awhile, just the two of us,
looking out across the water,
I said *yes.*

Rob Hunter

SEPTEMBER SWIM

Knee deep just feet from shore
your dive was more of an unhurried fall,

your hands ahead of you,
and then the water closed around your clothes,

your skirt collapsing suddenly
like a flower pulled by its stem through liquid.

You didn't make a sound.
The wind rustled leaves all around us

and corrugated the water.
The sun dipped lower.

I didn't know if you would ever
appear again because in that split second,

standing on the shore of this pond
in the mountains, long afternoon shadows

were black shrouds on the water,
tinges of yellow and orange already

seeping into leaves, I sensed the new season,
felt one season expire and pass on.

And in that moment you were submerged,
swallowed whole; but like a loon,

you bobbed up and shrieked the cold
baptism out of your lungs. You then stood up,

wet clothes clinging to your body,
your hands holding your surprised face.

Joyce Sutphen

WHAT TO DO

Wake up early, before the lights come on
in the houses on a street that was once
a farmer's field at the edge of a marsh.

Wander from room to room, hoping to find
words that could be enough to keep the soul
alive, words that might be useful or kind

in a world that is more wasteful and cruel
every day. Remind us that we are
like grass that fades, fleeting clouds in the sky,

and then give us just one of those moments
when we were paying attention, when we gave
up everything to see the world in

a grain of sand or to behold
a rainbow in the sky, the heart
leaping up.

William Stafford

ANY MORNING

Just lying on the couch and being happy.
Only humming a little, the quiet sound in the head.
Trouble is busy elsewhere at the moment, it has
so much to do in the world.

People who might judge are mostly asleep; they can't
monitor you all the time, and sometimes they forget.
When dawn flows over the hedge you can
get up and act busy.

Little corners like this, pieces of Heaven
left lying around, can be picked up and saved.
People won't even see that you have them,
they are so light and easy to hide.

Later in the day you can act like the others.
You can shake your head. You can frown.

Pieces of Heaven

It can be difficult to give yourself permission to do nothing and allow for the space from which a sudden gratefulness can naturally arise. We feel guilty for not tackling the tasks we "should" be doing or we worry that others will judge us if they catch us in the act of indulging what might feel like laziness. "Any Morning" by William Stafford offers a reprieve from the fear of judgment that can keep us from uncovering true joy in a simple moment spent alone. Though we might be busy, though we might be tempted to reach for our phones or some other distraction, this poem invites us to pause and embrace a bit of space before the day begins.

We can always seek out "little corners like this, pieces of Heaven" when we can just be ourselves, and do what makes us happy, even if that means "lying on the couch" and relishing a few minutes of soul time. We're often pressured to put on the frowning faces others wear in order to fit in, to fall in line with finding fault with the world or the people around us. But the more we take time for ourselves throughout each day, the less we feel obliged to act a certain way or complete a list of tasks just to please someone else.

Invitation for Writing and Reflection

What are your own "pieces of Heaven" that you'd like to pick up and save throughout the day? What are those secret things that bring you joy and keep hope alive, but which you worry others might judge?

Rosemerry Wahtola Trommer

HOW IT MIGHT CONTINUE

Wherever we go, the chance for joy,
whole orchards of amazement—

one more reason to always travel
with our pockets full of exclamation marks,

so we might scatter them for others
like apple seeds.

Some will dry out, some will blow away,
but some will take root

and grow exuberant groves
filled with long thin fruits

that resemble one hand clapping—
so much enthusiasm as they flutter back and forth

that although nothing's heard
and though nothing's really changed,

people everywhere for years to come
will swear that the world

is ripe with applause, will fill
their own pockets with new seeds to scatter.

Li-Young Lee

FROM BLOSSOMS

From blossoms comes
this brown paper bag of peaches
we bought from the boy
at the bend in the road where we turned toward
signs painted *Peaches.*

From laden boughs, from hands,
from sweet fellowship in the bins,
comes nectar at the roadside, succulent
peaches we devour, dusty skin and all,
comes the familiar dust of summer, dust we eat.

O, to take what we love inside,
to carry within us an orchard, to eat
not only the skin, but the shade,
not only the sugar, but the days, to hold
the fruit in our hands, adore it, then bite into
the round jubilance of peach.

There are days we live
as if death were nowhere
in the background; from joy
to joy to joy, from wing to wing,
from blossom to blossom to
impossible blossom, to sweet impossible blossom.

Jessica Gigot

MOTHERHOOD

When the lilacs come back
I remember that I was born,
That there was a robin's nest
Outside my mother's window
As she waited to count my toes.
Now her hands rest on her stomach
Tangled in contemplation
As if I am still in there.
Her fingers are woven together
Like a fisherman's net as she tries
One more time to offer advice.

Sarah Freligh

WONDROUS

I'm driving home from school when the radio talk
turns to E. B. White, his birthday, and I exit
the here and now of the freeway at rush hour,

travel back into the past, where my mother is reading
to my sister and me the part about Charlotte laying her eggs
and dying, and though this is the fifth time Charlotte

has died, my mother is crying again, and we're laughing
at her because we know nothing of loss and its sad math,
how every subtraction is exponential, how each grief

multiplies the one preceding it, how the author tried
seventeen times to record the words *She died alone*
without crying, seventeen takes and a short walk during

which he called himself ridiculous, a grown man crying
for a spider he'd spun out of the silk thread of invention—
wondrous how those words would come back and make

him cry, and, yes, wondrous to hear my mother's voice
ten years after the day she died—the catch, the rasp,
the gathering up before she could say to us, *I'm OK.*

Cathryn Essinger

SUMMER APPLES

I planted an apple tree in memory
of my mother, who is not gone,

but whose memory has become
so transparent that she remembers

slicing apples with her grandmother
(yellow apples; blue bowl) better than

the fruit that I hand her today. Still,
she polishes the surface with her thumb,

holds it to the light and says with no
hesitation, *Oh, Yellow Transparent . . .*

*they're so fragile, you can almost see
to the core.* She no longer remembers how

to roll the crust, sweeten the sauce, but
her desire is clear—it is pie that she wants.

And so, I slice as close as I dare to the core—
to that little cathedral to memory—where

the seeds remember everything they need
to know to become yellow and transparent.

Lynne Knight

THIRD YEAR OF MY MOTHER'S DEMENTIA

I looked out the window and it filled with peacocks,
flaring their many eyes at me. I had been waiting
for months for some sign, and now from the high bank
where I was so often afraid to climb blared cries

of the peacocks as they fluttered and dipped
their soft plumules. One lay down to sleep
like a human, positioned on its side, and its fan
folded back into itself, into nothing but a long

dull tail. The others kept moving up and down the bank,
so many eyes I could not count them. They ignored
the sleeping one. Stepped over him, or rushed by
with a swish. As they would rush by me, if I stood

among them in my wonder that beauty is needed
most of all when it is useless, when it fixes nothing.

Heather Swan

RABBIT

After a long numbness, I wake
and suddenly I'm noticing everything,
all of it piercing me with its beautiful,
radical trust: the carpenter bee tonguing
the needles of echinacea believing
in their sweetness, the exuberance
of an orange day lily unfolding itself
at the edge of the street, and the way
the moss knows the stone, and the stone
accepts its trespass, and the way the dog
on his leash turns to see if I'm holding on,
certain I know where to go. And the way
the baby rabbit—whose trembling ears
are the most delicate cups—trusts me,
because I pried the same dogs' jaws
off his hips, and then allows me to feed him
clover when his back legs no longer work,
forcing me to think about forgiveness
and those I need to forgive, and to hope
I am forgiven, and that just maybe
I can forgive myself. This unstoppable,
excruciating tenderness everywhere inviting
us, always inviting. And then later, the firefly
illuminating the lantern of its body,
like us, each time we laugh.

Dale Biron

LAUGHTER

When the
face we wear

grows old and weathered, torn
open by time,

colors
tinted as dawn

like the late
winter mountains

of Sedona
ashen and crimson,

it will no longer
be possible

to distinguish
our deepest scars

from the long
sweet lines left

by laughter.

January Gill O'Neil

IN THE COMPANY OF WOMEN

Make me laugh over coffee,
make it a double, make it frothy
so it seethes in our delight.
Make my cup overflow
with your small happiness.
I want to hoot and snort and cackle and chuckle.
Let your laughter fill me like a bell.
Let me listen to your ringing and singing
as Billie Holiday croons above our heads.
Sorry, the blues are nowhere to be found.
Not tonight. Not here.
No makeup. No tears.
Only contours. Only curves.
Each sip takes back a pound,
each dry-roasted swirl takes our soul.
Can I have a refill, just one more?
Let the bitterness sink to the bottom of our lives.
Let us take this joy to go.

Alice Wolf Gilborn

LEANING TO THE LIGHT

Our neighbor planted twelve
bulbs in the shadow of his barn
in the shadow of the trees
in the shadow of a mountain.
And now a dozen lilies grow
at an angle toward the sun
that touches them only
in the afternoon. Our neighbor
sold his house to strangers
who come for just a week
or two so they never see
their flowers bloom, later
than the rest, their soft pink
petals tinged with white,
curled like shavings, stamen
tuned to the western sky.
Like me since I left the land
where I was born, leaning west,
these laggard lilies with mouths wide
open, drinking in the setting sun.

Andrea Potos

I WATCHED AN ANGEL IN THE EMERGENCY ROOM

Tall in twilit
blue sneakers, feet winged
to the task of holding
my mother's hand as
he explained the source
of the infection, all it will take
to restore her
to the stronghold of
this earth that has known her
eight decades and more, the gate
of her body where my gratitude begins.

Alberto Ríos

WHEN GIVING IS ALL WE HAVE

One river gives
Its journey to the next.

We give because someone gave to us.
We give because nobody gave to us.

We give because giving has changed us.
We give because giving could have changed us.

We have been better for it,
We have been wounded by it—

Giving has many faces: It is loud and quiet,
Big, though small, diamond in wood-nails.

Its story is old, the plot worn and the pages too,
But we read this book, anyway, over and again:

Giving is, first and every time, hand to hand,
Mine to yours, yours to mine.

You gave me blue and I gave you yellow.
Together we are simple green. You gave me

What you did not have, and I gave you
What I had to give—together, we made

Something greater from the difference.

Albert Garcia

OFFERING

Here, take this palmful of raspberries
as my gift. It isn't much

but we've often said our needs
are simple, some quiet

time alone on the patio
in the cool morning, coffee,

a few words over the newspaper.
I've rinsed these berries

so you can tumble them
right into your cereal, one minute

on the vine, the next in your bowl,
my hand to your mouth.

Let's say my words were as simply
sweet as these berries, chosen

as carefully, plucked and held,
then delivered as perfect

morsels of meaning. Not
what you hear, which is never

what I mean to say. Will you take
these berries? Will you feel their weight

on your tongue, taste their tang
as they slide into you, small, bright, honest:

the only gift I have to give?

Alison Luterman

TOO MANY TO COUNT

My father hands me the bucket and scissors
and asks me to go cut peonies: white, pink, magenta.
Tightly balled and slightly unfurled,
they've multiplied like crazy on the slope behind his house.

Long ago, Dad taught himself to garden out of books.
My childhood was fat with exulted-over tomatoes,
blueberry bushes covered with cheesecloth,
and a zillion profligate zucchinis,
which caused an outbreak of zucchini bread,
zucchini muffins, and ill-fated zucchini pizza crust,
inciting both my brothers to go on a zucchini strike
that has lasted to this day.

But these peonies!
God must have been a little stoned when She dreamed
     them up,
not stopping at one petticoat or two,
but piling layer upon layer, until even the exhausted bees
surrender to excessive lingerie.
I stuff the bucket with closed buds
and half-opened blooms showing their lacy knickers
and trudge back up the steep-sloped hill to the house,

leaving behind a glowing field of peonies, too many to
    count,
like my father's many kindnesses over the decades—
pots of soup, loaves of home-baked bread,
hours of earnest listening,
all offered with the same voluptuous generosity
as now when he takes the laden bucket from my arms
and tells me to divide the bounty into smaller bunches
so he can distribute them among the neighbors.

Marjorie Saiser

IF I CARRY MY FATHER

I hope it is a little more
than color of hair
or the dimple or cheekbones
if he's ever here in the space I inhabit
the room I walk in
the boundaries and peripheries
I hope it's some kindness he believed in
living on in cell or bone
maybe some word or action
will float close to the surface
within my reach
some good will rise when I need it
a hard dense insoluble shard
will show up
and carry on.

George Bilgere

WEATHER

My father would lift me
to the ceiling in his big hands
and ask, *How's the weather up there?*
And it was good, the weather
of being in his hands, his breath
of scotch and cigarettes, his face
smiling from the world below.
O daddy, was the lullaby I sang
back down to him as he stood on earth,
my great, white-shirted father, home
from work, his gold wristwatch
and wedding band gleaming
as he held me above him
for as long as he could,
before his strength failed
down there in the world I find myself
standing in tonight, my little boy
looking down from his flight
below the ceiling, cradled in my hands,
his eyes wide and already staring
into the distance beyond the man
asking him again and again,
How's the weather up there?

Sally Bliumis-Dunn

WORK

I could tell they were father and son,
the air between them, slack as though
they hardly noticed one another.

The father sanded the gunwales,
the boy coiled the lines.
And I admired them there, each to his task

in the quiet of the long familiar.
The sawdust coated the father's arms
like dusk coats grass in a field.

The boy worked next on the oarlocks
polishing the brass until it gleamed
as though he could harness the sun.

Who cares what they were thinking,
lucky in their lives
that the spin of the genetic wheel

slowed twice to a stop
and landed each of them here.

The Joy of Making

Sally Bliumis-Dunn's "Work" shows two people steeped in the joy of what they're doing. They seem to be beaming, the fullness of their gratitude and good luck suddenly contagious.

We share her relief at watching this father and son build a boat together, disengaged from the technology that can disconnect us from each other. We all crave a creative outlet like this and can deeply enjoy being so involved in the task of making something that we lose all sense of time. In the space of creativity and cooperation, we also lose touch with our *self* for a while and shed those anxious thoughts that can be fed by social media and news.

This poem urges us to bear loving witness to the world as it is, to find beauty in the simple scene of a father and son coming together to accomplish something much larger than themselves. She points to "the spin of the genetic wheel" that led them, and each of us, to this very moment in our lives, and invites us to feel the luck of having become exactly who we are right now.

Invitation for Writing and Reflection

Can you remember a time when you felt so consumed with the act of making something that you lost all sense of time, and your mind seemed to clear? What allowed you to enter this mindful creative space?

Danusha Laméris

GOLDFINCHES

Good luck, they say,
to see one,
its face and breast
pure citrus
against the grey sky.

And today,
I am twice blessed
because two such birds
grace the low boughs
of the persimmon,
eating the soft heart
of winter's fruit—

though they will also
feast on thistles
pulled from the dry flowers
and so are said
to eat the thorns
of Christ's crown,
to lift some small measure
of his suffering.

Whatever your grief,
however long you've carried it—
may something
come to you,
quick and unexpected,
whisk away
the bristled edge
in its sharp
and tender beak.

Connie Wanek

THE LESSER GOLDFINCH

It was hardly bigger than an apricot,
a goldfinch, yes, but smaller and paler,
a little ghost in the lavender
eating seeds too tiny for
my old eyes. Sometimes I think
Heaven needn't measure
even two by two
inches, much less all the sky
above the Vatican;
for peace is lodged deep
within the very
spacious thought of itself.
Quiet bird, your gestures
are vast in such a place
as I dream of.

Tony Hoagland

THE WORD

Down near the bottom
of the crossed-out list
of things you have to do today,

between "green thread"
and "broccoli," you find
that you have penciled "sunlight."

Resting on the page, the word
is beautiful. It touches you
as if you had a friend

and sunlight were a present
he had sent from someplace distant
as this morning—to cheer you up,

and to remind you that,
among your duties, pleasure
is a thing

that also needs accomplishing.
Do you remember?
that time and light are kinds

of love, and love
is no less practical
than a coffee grinder

or a safe spare tire?
Tomorrow you may be utterly
without a clue,

but today you get a telegram
from the heart in exile,
proclaiming that the kingdom

still exists,
the king and queen alive,
still speaking to their children,

—to anyone among them
who can find the time
to sit out in the sun and listen.

Barbara Crooker

TOMORROW

there will be sun, scalloped by clouds,
ushered in by a waterfall of birdsong.
It will be a temperate seventy-five, low
humidity. For twenty-four hours,
all politicians will be silent. Reality
programs will vanish from TV, replaced
by the "snow" that used to decorate
our screens when reception wasn't
working. Soldiers will toss their weapons
in the grass. The oceans will stop
their inexorable rise. No one
will have to sit on a committee.
When twilight falls, the aurora borealis
will cut off cell phones, scramble the internet.
We'll play flashlight tag, hide and seek,
decorate our hair with fireflies, spin
until we're dizzy, collapse
on the dew-decked lawn and look up,
perhaps for the first time, to read the long lines
of cold code written in the stars . . .

Cynthia White

QUAIL HOLLOW

Think of the path as calligraphy—
narrow where it borders
the farm house and horse pens.

Think, how beyond the open gate,
the stroke fattens, traveling
upward into the dark

scrawl of live oak and bay.
See how the light
is a tender wash. Under

your feet, sand that once
cradled a sea. Blue-bellies skitter,
scritching like tiny scribes

among the leaves. Think
how little ink is required to write
three million years.

After the climb, the view,
the final loop. You pass the houses
of sleeping wood rats, the pond,

glassine slashed with cattails.
Now, before getting into your car,
consider with what ease

the rise and fall of robin song
can erase a certain ache,
the day's gathering premonitions.

Laura Grace Weldon

COMPOST HAPPENS

Nature teaches nothing is lost.
It's transmuted.

Spread between rows of beans,
last year's rusty leaves tamp down weeds.
Coffee grounds and banana peels
foster rose blooms. Bread crumbs
scattered for birds become song.
Leftovers offered to chickens come back
as eggs, yolks sunrise orange.
Broccoli stems and bruised apples
fed to cows return as milk steaming in the pail,
as patties steaming in the pasture.

Surely our shame and sorrow
also return,
composted by years
into something generative as wisdom.

Joan Mazza

PART OF THE LANDSCAPE

An old wooden bench, aging gray, colonized
by moss, liverworts, and lichens that drape
the surface, where I rest along my woodland
walks, wear clothes to match the earthy landscape—
grays and greens and browns, a mottled muddle
so I don't stand out. After two weeks, crows
don't scream to warn the neighborhood, but huddle
with their kind to chat. As still as possible,
I am a rock, a tree. Nothing flees from me.
Near my head, a golden crowned kinglet, smaller
than a chickadee or chipping sparrow.
I hold still, photograph this world with just
my eyes, forget the news. My heart is here,
filled with gratitude as I fade and disappear.

Andrea Potos

ESSENTIAL GRATITUDE

Sometimes it just stuns you
like an arrow flung from some angel's wing.
Sometimes it hastily scribbles
a list in the air: black coffee,
thick new books,
your pillow's cool underside,
the quirky family you married into.

It is content with so little really;
even the ink of your pen along
the watery lines of your dimestore notebook
could be a swiftly moving prayer.

The Gratitude List

As Andrea Potos's "Essential Gratitude" points out, the sensation of appreciation can come out of nowhere and pierce our hearts until we find ourselves making a whole list "in the air" of those everyday things we might otherwise look past or ignore. One of the most potent practices we can adopt is including a gratitude list as part of our journaling or writing practice, in the morning or at night before bed. Turning the mind toward reverence through our writing can ensure that a grateful attitude becomes a habit and follows us wherever we go.

By regularly listing the elements of this ordinary, miraculous life as concrete lines on the page, we ensure that we move through our days looking for reasons to be happy. Potos also reminds us that saying a simple thank you can be its own kind of prayer, whether it happens out loud or follows "the watery lines of your dimestore notebook."

Invitation for Writing and Reflection

The next time a sudden feeling of appreciation "stuns" you, take the time to write out your own gratitude list as soon as possible. When you pay attention, what specific sensory details about this grateful moment stand out to you as worthy of praise?

Laura Foley

GRATITUDE LIST

Praise be this morning for sleeping late,
the sandy sheets, the ocean air,
the midnight storm that blew its waters in.
Praise be the morning swim, mid-tide,
the clear sands underneath our feet,
the dogs who leap into the waves,
their fur, sticky with salt,
the ball we throw again and again.
Praise be the green tea with honey,
the bread we dip in finest olive oil,
the eggs we fry. Praise be the reeds,
gold and pink in the summer light,
the sand between our toes,
our swimsuits, flapping in the breeze.

Katherine Williams

THE DOG BODY OF MY SOUL

Some days I feel
like a retriever
racing
back and forth
fetching the tired
old balls
the universe
tosses me.

Some days
I'm on a leash
following
someone else's
route,
sensing
I'm supposed
to be grateful.

Some days
I'm waiting
in a darkened
house
bladder insistent
not knowing
when my people
will return.

But some days
I hurl myself
into the sweet
stinging surf,
race wildly back
and roll
in the sand's
warm welcome.

Katie Rubinstein

SCRATCH, SNIFF

It was weeks ago now
that first September I spent here on this island,
still hot and balmy.
I wanted a scratch and sniff for you,
some clever little corner of the screen
so I could share this most perfect thing:
the smell of beach roses, all briney.

They were abundant outside of the cottage,
and each time I passed, I wondered how I'd gotten so lucky—
that they became like dandelions in my life.

Hardy, scrappy and perfectly soft all at the same time,
nestled in their rocky, sandy homes, smelling like heaven—
those round, round hips.
I wanted to eat them, be them,

and I wanted you to smell them
as if sharing them would somehow
exponentially increase the delight
or make the sense more real.

But it was mine alone
and exquisite all the same.

Mary Elder Jacobsen

SUMMER COTTAGE

I'm halfway through a day
that began like a gift
in a blue china eggcup
set on the table before me
by my grandma at the shore
always awake before sunup
always beginning it for me
her soft tap-tap-tapping,
her careful cracking to open
what seemed a rare jewel box
how she raised its little lid
let me peek past the edge
let me see the whole horizon
orbiting the yolk-yellow sun
how brightly it would glisten
hovering there just for me.

Jane Kenyon

COMING HOME AT TWILIGHT IN LATE SUMMER

We turned into the drive,
and gravel flew up from the tires
like sparks from a fire. So much
to be done—the unpacking, the mail
and papers . . . the grass needed mowing . . .
We climbed stiffly out of the car.
The shut-off engine ticked as it cooled.

And then we noticed the pear tree,
the limbs so heavy with fruit
they nearly touched the ground.
We went out to the meadow; our steps
made black holes in the grass;
and we each took a pear,
and ate, and were grateful.

Grace Bauer

PERCEPTIVE PRAYER

The beauty of summer nights
is how they go on—
light lingering so long we can
imagine ourselves immortal.
For moments at a time.

And winter days—
their own kind of beauty.
Any swatch of color:
hint of leaf bud, sway
of dried brown grass, even litter—

a bright yellow bag
light enough for the breeze
to lift and carry,
can render itself as pleasure
to an eye immersed in gray.

May we learn to love
what is both
ordinary and extra.
May our attention be
a kind of praise.
A worship of the all
there really is.

Patricia Fontaine

SAP ICICLES

On the row
of fresh pruned maples
along Bostwick Road
the cold wind
froze sap icicles sideways.
I saw a chickadee
land at an icicle tip,
so I pulled over
and put my tongue
to the cold tears of the tree.
Tasted flint,
tasted maple steam
when it rises off the pan,
tasted the shimmer
pulsing up inside
the cool grey bark
as the sun applies
its long March hands.

The happiest child in me
was tongued to that tree,
while the saddest
grieved the lost limbs.

On the side of the road
we grew up inside
my black coat, became
white-haired,
cared nothing
for the gawping cars.

Lucille Clifton

the lesson of the falling leaves

the leaves believe
such letting go is love
such love is faith
such faith is grace
such grace is god
i agree with the leaves

Ted Kooser

A DERVISH OF LEAVES

Sometimes when I'm sad, the dead leaves
in the bed of my pickup get up on their own
and start dancing. I'll be driving along,
glance up at the mirror and there they'll be,
swirling and bowing, their flying skirts
brushing the back window, not putting a hand
on the top of the cab to steady themselves,
but daringly leaning out over the box,
making fun of the fence posts we're passing
who have never left home, teasing the rocks
rolled away into the ditches, leaves light
in their slippers, dancing around in the back
of my truck, tossing their cares to the wind,
sometimes, when I'm down in my heart.

James Crews

WINTER MORNING

When I can no longer say thank you
for this new day and the waking into it,
for the cold scrape of the kitchen chair
and the ticking of the space heater glowing
orange as it warms the floor near my feet,
I know it is because I've been fooled again
by the selfish, unruly man who lives in me
and believes he deserves only safety
and comfort. But if I pause as I do now,
and watch the streetlights outside winking
off one by one like old men closing their
cloudy eyes, if I listen to my tired neighbors
slamming car doors hard against the morning
and see the steaming coffee in their mugs
kissing their chapped lips as they sip and
exhale each of their worries white into
the icy air around their faces—then I can
remember this one life is a gift each of us
was handed and told to open: Untie the bow
and tear off the paper, look inside
and be grateful for whatever you find
even if it is only the scent of a tangerine
that lingers on the fingers long after
you've finished peeling it.

Tracy K. Smith

THE GOOD LIFE

When some people talk about money
They speak as if it were a mysterious lover
Who went out to buy milk and never
Came back, and it makes me nostalgic
For the years I lived on coffee and bread,
Hungry all the time, walking to work on payday
Like a woman journeying for water
From a village without a well, then living
One or two nights like everyone else
On roast chicken and red wine.

Marjorie Saiser

THANKSGIVING FOR TWO

The adults we call our children will not be arriving
with their children in tow for Thanksgiving.
We must make our feast ourselves,

slice our half-ham, indulge, fill our plates,
potatoes and green beans
carried to our table near the window.

We are the feast, plenty of years,
arguments. I'm thinking the whole bundle of it
rolls out like a white tablecloth. We wanted

to be good company for one another.
Little did we know that first picnic
how this would go. Your hair was thick,

mine long and easy; we climbed a bluff
to look over a storybook plain. We chose
our spot as high as we could, to see

the river and the checkerboard fields.
What we didn't see was this day, in
our pajamas if we want to,

wrinkled hands strong, wine
in juice glasses, toasting
whatever's next,

the decades of side-by-side,
our great good luck.

The Feast of Each Moment

It's difficult to resist the social pressure that turns the holidays into an excuse for consumption and a source of stress. Yet in "Thanksgiving for Two," Marjorie Saiser brings love and acceptance to a situation that might anger or disappoint other parents: Her children will not be coming home for the holiday this year. Even in the first line, she acknowledges that they are adults with lives and children of their own, and we sense a hint of relief that she and her husband will get to "indulge" alone and reminisce about "that first picnic" that led them to this day together. Saiser reminds us that when we "make our feast ourselves," we transform the holidays back into holy days that focus on joy and deeper connection; we allow the abundance of our lives to roll out "like a white tablecloth," full of countless blessings laid out for us.

Invitation for Writing and Reflection

Describe a time when you turned what might have been a difficult or disappointing situation into your own feast, making the most of it. What allowed you to generate a thankful, hopeful attitude in those moments, to recognize even the smallest gifts in the midst of a challenge?

Jeffrey Harrison

NEST

It wasn't until we got the Christmas tree
into the house and up on the stand
that our daughter discovered a small bird's nest
tucked among its needled branches.

Amazing, that the nest had made it
all the way from Nova Scotia on a truck
mashed together with hundreds of other trees
without being dislodged or crushed.

And now it made the tree feel wilder,
a balsam fir growing in our living room,
as though at any moment a bird might flutter
through the house and return to the nest.

And yet, because we'd brought the tree indoors,
we'd turned the nest into the first ornament.
So we wound the tree with strings of lights,
draped it with strands of red beads,

and added the other ornaments, then dropped
two small brass bells into the nest, like eggs
containing music, and hung a painted goldfinch
from the branch above, as if to keep them warm.

Ellen Bass

GETTING INTO BED ON A DECEMBER NIGHT

When I slip beneath the quilt and fold into
her warmth, I think we are like the pages
of a love letter written thirty years ago
that some aging god still reads each day
and then tucks back into its envelope.

Lisa Coffman

EVERYBODY MADE SOUPS

After it all, the events of the holidays,
the dinner tables passing like great ships,
everybody made soups for a while.
Cooked and cooked until the broth kept
the story of the onion, the weeping meat.
It was over, the year was spent, the new one
had yet to make its demands on us,
each day lay in the dark like a folded letter.
Then out of it all we made one final thing
out of the bounty that had not always filled us,
out of the ruined cathedral carcass of the turkey,
the limp celery chopped back into plenty,
the fish head, the spine. Out of the rejected,
the passed over, never the object of love.
It was as if all the pageantry had been for this:
the quiet after, the simmered light,
the soothing shapes our mouths made as we tasted.

James Crews

DARKEST BEFORE DAWN

Three days into the new year,
and despite the lack of adequate light,
our white phalaenopsis orchid
has eased open a third delicate bloom.
Perhaps coaxed by the warmth
of the woodstove a few feet away,
the orchid thrives in its tiny pot
shaped like the shell of a nautilus,
sending out new stems and glossy leaves,
its aerial roots—green at the tips—
reaching upward like tentacles
to sip the morning air. These blooms
stir something too long asleep in me,
proving with stillness and slow growth
what I haven't been able to trust
these past few months—that hope
and grace still reign in certain sectors
of the living world, that there are laws
which can never be overturned
by hateful words or the wishes
of power-hungry men. Be patient,
this orchid seems to say, and reveal
your deepest self even in the middle
of winter, even in the darkness
before the coming dawn.

Brad Peacock

ROSARY

for my grandfather

Some say it is darkest before dawn—
they must not be morning dwellers,
those of us who wake
long before the masses
to see the beauty
of a world in transition.
I walk these city streets
stripped of yesterday's worries,
laid bare like the sidewalks in front of me.
A crow calls
stopping me in my tracks,
back to the here and now,
after my mind has taken flight.
I look toward the sky
for the sentinel to sound his alarm again,
and glimpse a sliver of silver light
illuminating the cross
atop a towering cathedral.
I feel my fingers move in my mittens,
as if tracing every detail
of those sacred family beads
you handed me
long before you were gone.

Julie Murphy

TO ASK

To wear your dead husband's sweatshirt
long after his scent has faded,
the cotton soft, wrist and waist bands
frayed, the white *Wrigley Field*
still bright, to pull the hood over your head,
nestle into darkness the way he would on a cold night,
to conjure him, slideshow of your lives
playing in the background, shot by shot,
as if this cloth could incarnate the self
who wore it, day after day, year after year,
or the self who you were, to be that self for an instant,
glimpse whatever it was—joy, sorrow—
that made you whole,
to know yourself forever changed,
glimpse or no glimpse, gone forever.
To not know, in the vast space
of grief, who you ever could become,
and ask who, without despair
to ask with hope—

Tess Taylor

THERE DOESN'T NEED TO BE A POEM

for this sadness. Simply to breathe
next to a stream that slips into the gutter
near your house

would be enough. To see,
next door, in the graveyard,
the brown-and-yellow millipede

bury itself below one granite stone,
joining in the work of making soil,
just as now the faithful oxygen

still turns the copper headstone green,
oxidizing to patina despite all.
By luck, your own feathered alveoli

still redden blood, your fine cell walls
trade oxygen for carbon,
and sift the windy mix we call the air:

This happens, going on invisibly
even if no one remembers how
& even if it seems that pain

is a volatile molecule, grief
bonding unpredictably to things.
Now the late sun rims a cloud.

You, who watch that cloud:
Inhale. Exhale.

Amy Dryansky

WINGSPAN

for Donna

Every day I draw in air you can't
& try to send it to you, alone
in a hospital, a machine breathing
for you, & because we aren't
allowed to see you I'm imagining
wings for you—yes, cynical me
earnestly conjuring an angel
or eagle, golden, wings spread,
alighting immensely gently
on your chest, carrying light & air
from my lungs, from the many
who love you, filling your lungs
with breath, heat, life, a garden.
If I could, I would wake you
with light, believe in anything.

Joy Harjo

EAGLE POEM

To pray you open your whole self
To sky, to earth, to sun, to moon
To one whole voice that is you.
And know there is more
That you can't see, can't hear;
Can't know except in moments
Steadily growing, and in languages
That aren't always sound but other
Circles of motion.
Like eagle that Sunday morning
Over Salt River. Circled in blue sky
In wind, swept our hearts clean
With sacred wings.
We see you, see ourselves and know
That we must take the utmost care
And kindness in all things.
Breathe in, knowing we are made of
All this, and breathe, knowing
We are truly blessed because we
Were born, and die soon within a
True circle of motion,
Like eagle rounding out the morning
Inside us.
We pray that it will be done
In beauty.
In beauty.

Terri Kirby Erickson

WHAT MATTERS

What other people think of you,
what they say, are burdens
no one should carry. Lift a spoon,

a cup, things that fit in your hand.
Carry on a conversation,
pick up a baby. Listen to the wind

when it whispers, nothing else.
There is no one watching you,
no one straining to hear what

you say. The present has arrived
and you are in it. Your heart
is pumping. Your breath moves

in and out of your lungs without
anyone's help or permission.
Let go of everything else. Let

your life, handed to you through
no effort of your own, be all
the proof you need. You are loved.

Mark Nepo

IN LOVE WITH THE WORLD

There is no end to love. We may tear ourselves away, or fall off the cliff we thought sacred, or return one day to find the home we dreamt of burning. But when the rain slows to a slant and the pavement turns cold, that place where I keep you and you and all of you—that place opens, like a fist no longer strong enough to stay closed. And the ache returns. Thank God. The sweet and sudden ache that lets me know I am alive. The rain keeps misting my face. What majesty of cells assembles around this luminous presence that moves around as me? How is it I'm still here? Each thing touched, each breath, each glint of light, each pain in my gut is cause for praise. I pray to keep falling in love with everyone I meet, with every child's eye, with every fallen being getting up. Like a worm cut in two, the heart only grows another heart. When the cut in my mind heals, I grow another mind. Birds migrate and caribou circle the cold top of the world. Perhaps we migrate between love and suffering, making our wounded-joyous cries: alone, then together, alone, then together. Oh praise the soul's migration. I fall. I get up. I run from you. I look for you. I am again in love with the world.

READING GROUP QUESTIONS AND TOPICS FOR DISCUSSION

"In Any Event" by Dorianne Laux (page 10)

- Does this strike you as a hopeful poem, and if so, why?
- What do you think Laux means when she says, "there is something more to come for humanity," and when she refers to the heart as "an uncharted sea"?
- In the end, the poet implies that the praise she applies to humanity will help lift us all up, in spite of our flaws. How might praise of a difficult situation lead to acceptance and gratitude?
- **INVITATION FOR WRITING AND REFLECTION:** When was the last time you felt a full faith in the goodness and potential of humanity, when you felt truly grateful to be alive? What brought on this feeling?

"Hoodie" by January Gill O'Neil (page 20)

- Why does this mother thinking of her son "fear for his safety," and what is significant about the image of his hoodie in the poem?
- Consider the final lines, when this mother wonders "who could mistake him / for anything but good." How might these words invite us into a sense of greater compassion?
- What are some of the ways that O'Neil's poem urges us to hold on to the basic assumption of goodness and innocence in others, no matter what they might be wearing, no matter the color of their skin?

- INVITATION FOR WRITING AND REFLECTION: Describe an instance when you were able to see past your own anxieties and come into a deeper empathy with others in your world. What allowed you to scale the wall of fear, and how did it feel to move toward the hope on the other side?

"A Cure Against Poisonous Thought" by Annie Lighthart (page 35)

- What is the "cure" that Lighthart presents here as she observes a bee bending inside a honeysuckle blossom?
- How can the simple act of observation, especially in nature, lift us out of our minds?
- What do you make of the last lines of the poem? How is the body "not root but wick," always searching for "the press of light" that she mentions?
- INVITATION FOR WRITING AND REFLECTION: Describe a time when a moment spent in the natural world helped pause your thoughts and made you feel more fully alive.

"The Fish" by Jane Hirshfield (page 53)

- In this poem, Hirshfield suggests there is some part of us, fishlike, "that stitches / the inner water / and the outer water together." Do you feel there is some part of us that constantly swims between inner and outer worlds to fulfill our needs?
- What do you feel she means when she says, "we walk the luminous seam"? Must we always tread the line between our mind and life as it is around us?

- Do you agree that there's a "broad world we make daily" in our minds, and one we "daily give ourselves to"? Is she implying that we create the world we live in, to a large degree, yet must still surrender to certain aspects of reality that remain out of our control?
- INVITATION FOR WRITING AND REFLECTION: If we take enough time for ourselves (and for our souls), we can sometimes "flow" between self and world, perhaps even enjoying the back and forth. Think back to a time when you walked "the luminous seam" with more ease and consider what allowed you to do so.

"How It Might Continue" by Rosemerry Wahtola Trommer (page 94)

- What does Trommer mean when she suggests that we can go around with "our pockets full of exclamation marks"? Do you know someone like this, who carries the seeds of delight with them wherever they go, giving them freely?
- Do you find that amazement and joy can be contagious? How might you make it a daily practice to "scatter" and spread that joy to others, even knowing that some of the seeds will not grow?
- How can our own joy bring about change in the world, even if it's not "heard," even if the change is not tangible?
- INVITATION FOR WRITING AND REFLECTION: When was the last time you gave yourself permission to fully feel an instance of joy or amazement? Did this feeling catch on with others and carry over into other areas of your life?

"When Giving Is All We Have" by Alberto Ríos
(page 105)

- In this poem, Ríos implies that we give to one another, whether we directly benefit or not. Why is it important to keep giving, even if we end up wounded or feel that there was no point?

- How can giving be both loud and quiet, big and small? What do you think the poet means when he says that generosity can be like "diamond in wood-nails"?

- Toward the poem's end, Ríos says that when we each give what we have to offer, we all come up with something that is "greater from the difference." How so? Does what he's saying here apply to any current political situations?

- INVITATION FOR WRITING AND REFLECTION: What are some of the many small and large ways that you give to others on a daily basis, loved ones and strangers alike?

"Compost Happens" by Laura Grace Weldon
(page 122)

- Weldon describes how kitchen scraps turn back into roses, birdsong, and eggs. How else does nature remind us that everything changes, and "nothing is lost"?

- What are some of the images that stand out to you in this poem, and why?

- Do you think the poet is urging us to embrace difficult emotions like shame or sorrow? How might they eventually come back to us as wisdom or gratitude?

- INVITATION FOR WRITING AND REFLECTION: What experiences (shame, sorrow, anger, regret) would you "compost" if you could? You might begin each new sentence with the phrase, "I'd compost" and see where that leads as you practice trusting that no feeling is ever wasted.

"Gratitude List" by Laura Foley (page 126)

- In this poem, Foley seems to be describing a family vacation. How does the repeating phrase "praise be" add to the power of the poem?
- The word "praise" is usually associated with religious contexts. How would you define praise?
- Even though the poem unfolds as a gratitude list, how does Foley bring us more deeply into these moments with her choice of specific images?
- INVITATION FOR WRITING AND REFLECTION: Describe a particular time in your own life—a vacation perhaps, or just a lazy Sunday—for which you felt deeply grateful. See if you can recreate all the vivid details from that day, and you might start by using the same phrase, "Praise be," to begin each new sentence.

"Everybody Made Soups" by Lisa Coffman
(page 144)

- Many of us make soups throughout winter to bring nourishment and warmth to the long days. What brings gratitude and comfort to you during the winter months or during challenging times in your life?
- Which descriptions of food in the poem particularly stand out to you?

- How does Coffman suggest that the act of making a soup is somehow redeeming, making use of all the leftovers to create that "simmered light"?
- INVITATION FOR WRITING AND REFLECTION: This poem seems reminiscent of the Danish word *hygge* (pronounced "hoo-ga"), which refers to something that offers a quality of coziness, comfort, and well-being. What gives you *hygge* in the depths of winter, or on days when you feel especially dull?

"Eagle Poem" by Joy Harjo (page 151)

- How is Harjo, writing from the perspective of a Native American, inviting us to widen our definition of prayer in this poem?
- What are some of the ways her images tie us to the natural world, and those "circles of motion" of which she implies we are all a part?
- What do you think Harjo means when she urges readers to "open your whole self . . . to one whole voice that is you"? How does this poem-prayer ultimately become an expression of gratitude for the blessing of life?
- INVITATION FOR WRITING AND REFLECTION: Toward the middle of the poem, Harjo describes the eagle she saw one Sunday morning above a river and says the vision "swept our hearts clean / with sacred wings." In conversation or in your journal, describe a similar experience you've had with the natural world, which felt sacred and cleansing to you.

POET BIOGRAPHIES

Lahab Assef Al-Jundi was born and raised in Damascus, Syria. After graduating from the University of Texas in Austin with a degree in electrical engineering, he discovered his passion for writing and published his first poetry collection, *A Long Way*, in 1985. His latest collection is *No Faith at All* (Pecan Grove Press, 2014). He lives in San Antonio.

Ellen Bass is a chancellor of the Academy of American Poets and author, most recently, of *Indigo* (Copper Canyon Press, 2020). Her books include *Like a Beggar* (2014), *The Human Line* (2007), and *Mules of Love* (BOA Editions, 2002), which won the Lambda Literary Award. She coedited (with Florence Howe) the first major anthology of women's poetry, *No More Masks!* (Doubleday, 1973), and founded poetry workshops at the Salinas Valley State Prison and the Santa Cruz jails.

Grace Bauer is the author of five collections of poems, plus several chapbooks. *Unholy Heart: New & Selected Poems* is forthcoming from the University of Nebraska Press/ Backwaters.

George Bilgere's collections include *Blood Pages* (University of Pittsburgh Press, 2018), *Imperial, The White Museum, Haywire, The Good Kiss, Big Bang*, and *The Going*. Bilgere has received the *New Ohio Review* Editor's Choice Poetry Award, the Midland Authors Prize, the May Swenson Poetry Award, a Pushcart Prize, a grant from the National Endowment for the Arts, a Fulbright Fellowship, a Witter Bynner Fellowship, and the Cleveland Arts Prize. His work has appeared in *Poetry, Kenyon Review, Ploughshares, Southern Review, Best American Poetry, Georgia Review, Hopkins Quarterly*, and elsewhere. He teaches at John Carroll University in Cleveland, Ohio.

Dale Biron is a poet, an author, a speaker, and a professor. He has presented and taught classes in many venues, including TEDx Marin, Herbst Theatre, Moveon, and OLLI Dominican University. He served on the Marin Poetry Center board and was past poetry editor for A Network for Grateful Living. He is the author of a book of collected poems, *Why We Do Our Daily Practices* (2014), and his latest prose book is *Poetry for the Leader Inside You: A Search and Rescue Mission for the Heart and Soul* (2018).

Sally Bliumis-Dunn teaches modern poetry at Manhattanville College and the Palm Beach Poetry Festival. Her poems have appeared in *New Ohio Review, On the Seawall, The Paris Review, Prairie Schooner, PLUME, Poetry London, New York Times,* and *upstreet,* and on PBS NewsHour, The Writer's Almanac, Academy of American Poets Poem-a-Day,

and American Life in Poetry, among others. Her books include *Talking Underwater* (Wind Publications, 2007), *Second Skin* (2010), *Galapagos Poems* (Kattywompus Press, 2016), and *Echolocation* (Madhat Press, 2018).

Laure-Anne Bosselaar is the author of *The Hour Between Dog and Wolf, Small Gods of Grief,* which won the Isabella Gardner Prize for Poetry, and *A New Hunger,* selected as a Notable Book by the American Library Association. Winner of the 2020 James Dickey Prize for Poetry and the recipient of a Pushcart Prize, she is the editor of four anthologies and a member of the founding faculty at the Solstice MFA in Creative Writing. Her latest collection is *These Many Rooms* (Four Way Books). She is Santa Barbara poet laureate (2019-2021).

Abigail Carroll is the author of *Habitation of Wonder; A Gathering of Larks: Letters to Saint Francis from a Modern-Day Pilgrim;* and *Three*

Squares: The Invention of the American Meal. Carroll's poems have appeared in *Crab Orchard Review, Midwest Quarterly, Sojourners, Terrain,* and the anthology *Between Midnight and Dawn: A Literary Guide to Prayer for Lent, Holy Week, and Eastertide* (Paraclete Press, 2016). She serves as pastor of arts and spiritual formation at Church at the Well in Burlington, Vermont, and enjoys weaving, playing Celtic harp, and walking the pastures behind her farmhouse.

Kristen Case's poetry collections include *Little Arias* (New Issues Press, 2015) and *Principles of Economics* (Switchback Books, 2018), which won the Gatewood Prize. She is the recipient of a MacDowell Fellowship and has twice been awarded the Maine Literary Award in poetry. Case is also the author of numerous scholarly essays and is coeditor of the volumes *Thoreau at 200: Essays and Reassessments* (Cambridge, 2016) and *21|19: Contemporary Poets in the 19th Century Archive* (Milkweed Editions). She teaches American literature at the University of Maine at Farmington.

Judith Chalmer is the author of two collections of poems, *Minnow* (Kelsay Books, 2020) and *Out of History's Junk Jar* (Time Being Books, 1995). She is cotranslator of two books of haiku and tanka with Michiko Oishi: *Red Fish Alphabet* (Honami Syoten, 2008) and *Deepening Snow* (Plowboy Press, 2012). She was director of VSA Vermont, a nonprofit in arts and disability. In 2018 she received the Arthur Williams Award from the Vermont Arts Council for Meritorious Service in the Arts. She lives with her partner, Lisa, in Vermont.

Lucille Clifton (1936–2010) authored many collections of poetry, including *Blessing the Boats: New and Selected Poems 1988–2000* (BOA Editions, 2000), which won the National Book Award; *Good Woman: Poems and a Memoir 1969–1980* (BOA Editions,

1987), which was nominated for the Pulitzer Prize; and *Two-Headed Woman* (University of Massachusetts Press, 1980), also a Pulitzer Prize nominee as well as the recipient of the University of Massachusetts Press Juniper Prize. Her honors include an Emmy Award from the American Academy of Television Arts and Sciences, a Lannan Literary Award, two fellowships from the National Endowment for the Arts, and the 2007 Ruth Lilly Prize.

Lisa Coffman's work has been featured on The Writer's Almanac and BBC News, in the *Oxford American, Village Voice, Philadelphia Inquirer,* and elsewhere. She is the author of *Likely* and *Less Obvious Gods* and has been awarded the Stan and Tom Wick Poetry Prize from Kent State University Press and fellowships from the National Endowment for the Arts, Pew Charitable Trusts, and Bucknell University's Stadler Center for Poetry. She collaborated with composer Timothy Melbinger on the six-poem cycle *Hymns to Less*

Obvious Gods, which premiered in spring 2019.

James Crews is the author of four collections of poetry: *The Book of What Stays, Telling My Father, Bluebird,* and *Every Waking Moment.* He is also the editor of the anthology *Healing the Divide: Poems of Kindness and Connection.* He lives with his husband in Shaftsbury, Vermont, and teaches creative writing privately and at the University at Albany. jamescrews.net

Barbara Crooker is a poetry editor for *Italian-Americana,* and the author of nine books of poetry; *Some Glad Morning* (University of Pittsburgh Press, 2019) is the latest. Her awards include the W. B. Yeats Society of New York Award, Thomas Merton Poetry of the Sacred Award, and three Pennsylvania Council on the Arts Creative Writing Fellowships. Her work appears in literary journals and anthologies, including *The Valparaiso Poetry Review, The Chariton Poetry Review, Green Mountains Review,*

Tar River Poetry Review, The Beloit Poetry Journal, The Denver Quarterly, Smartish Pace, Gargoyle, The American Poetry Journal, Dogwood, Passages North, Nimrod, The Bedford Introduction to Literature, Nasty Women: An Unapologetic Anthology of Subversive Verse, and has been read on ABC, the BBC, The Writer's Almanac, and featured in American Life in Poetry.

Noah Davis grew up in Tipton, Pennsylvania, and writes about the Allegheny Front. Davis's manuscript *Of This River* was selected by George Ella Lyon for the 2019 Wheelbarrow Emerging Poet Book Prize from Michigan State University's Center for Poetry. His poems and prose have appeared in *The SUN, Best New Poets, Orion, North American Review, River Teeth, Sou'wester*, and *Chautauqua*, among others. He was awarded a Katharine Bakeless Nason Fellowship at the Bread Loaf Writers' Conference, and the 2018 Jean Ritchie Appalachian Literature Fellowship from

Lincoln Memorial University. Davis earned an MFA from Indiana University and now lives with his wife, Nikea, in Missoula, Montana.

Todd Davis is the author of six collections of poetry, most recently *Native Species, Winterkill*, and *In the Kingdom of the Ditch*, all published by Michigan State University Press. He has won Foreword INDIES Book of the Year bronze and silver awards, the Gwendolyn Brooks Poetry Prize, the Chautauqua Editors Prize, and the Bloomsburg University Book Prize. His poems have appeared in *Alaska Quarterly Review, American Poetry Review, Gettysburg Review, Iowa Review, Missouri Review, North American Review, Orion*, and *Poetry Northwest*. He teaches environmental studies, American literature, and creative writing at Pennsylvania State University's Altoona College.

Amy Dryansky has published two poetry collections; *Grass Whistle* (Salmon Poetry)

received the Massachusetts Book Award, and *How I Got Lost So Close to Home* won the New England/New York Award from Alice James. Her work is included in several anthologies and in *Barrow Street, Harvard Review, New England Review, Memorious, Orion, The SUN, Tin House*, and other journals. She's received honors from the Massachusetts Cultural Council, MacDowell Colony, and the Bread Loaf Writers' Conference, and is the former poet laureate of Northampton, Massachusetts. She directs the Culture, Brain, and Development Program at Hampshire College and parents two children. amydryansky.com

Jehanne Dubrow is the author of nine poetry collections, including *Wild Kingdom* (Louisiana State University Press, 2021) and *Simple Machines*, winner of the Richard Wilbur Poetry Award, and a book of creative nonfiction, *throughsmoke: an essay in notes*. Her work has appeared in *Poetry, New England Review*, and *The Southern Review*. She is professor of creative writing at the University of North Texas.

Terri Kirby Erickson is the author of six collections, including *Becoming the Blue Heron* (Press 53) and *A Sun Inside My Chest*. Her work has appeared in American Life in Poetry, *Asheville Poetry Review, Atlanta Review, Healing the Divide: Poems of Kindness and Connection, Connotation Press, JAMA, Latin American Literary Review, Plainsongs, Poetry Foundation, Poet's Market, storySouth, The Christian Century, The SUN, Valparaiso Poetry Review, Verse Daily*, and many others. Her awards include the Joy Harjo Poetry Prize, the Atlanta Review International Publication Prize, the Nazim Hikmet Poetry Award, and a Nautilus Silver Book Award. She lives in North Carolina.

Cathryn Essinger is the author of four books of poetry, including *The Apricot and the Moon* (Dos Madres Press, 2020). A chapbook titled *Wings*, about raising monarch butterflies, is forthcoming. Her poems have appeared in *Poetry, River Styx,* and *PANK* and have been featured on The Writer's Almanac and in American Life in Poetry. She lives in Troy, Ohio, where she raises monarch butterflies and tries to live up to her dog's expectations. cathrynessinger.com

Patricia Fargnoli was born in Hartford, Connecticut. A retired psychotherapist, she began studying poetry in her mid-thirties. Her first book, *Necessary Light* (Utah State University Press, 1999), was published when she was 62. Fargnoli served as New Hampshire poet laureate from 2006 to 2009 and was associate editor of the *Worcester Review.* Awards include an honorary BFA from the New Hampshire Institute of Arts and a MacDowell fellowship. She resides in Walpole, New Hampshire.

Farnaz Fatemi is an Iranian American writer and editor in Santa Cruz, California. She is a member and cofounder of the Hive Poetry Collective (hivepoetry.org). Her poetry and prose appear in *SWWIM Daily, Grist Journal, Catamaran Literary Reader, Crab Orchard Review, Tahoma Literary Review, Tupelo Quarterly,* and several anthologies, including *My Shadow Is My Skin: Voices from the Iranian Diaspora* and *The BreakBeat Poets Vol. 3: Halal If You Hear Me.* She taught writing at the University of California, Santa Cruz, from 1997–2018. farnazfatemi.com

Molly Fisk, as an Academy of American Poets Laureate Fellow, recently edited *California Fire and Water: A Climate Crisis Anthology.* She's the author of *The More Difficult Beauty, Listening to Winter,* and *Houston, We Have a Possum* among other books, and has won grants from the National Endowment for the Arts, the California Arts Council, and the Corporation for Public Broadcasting. Fisk lives in the Sierra foothills, where she teaches writing to cancer patients, provides weekly commentary to community radio, and works as a radical life coach. patreon.com/mollyfisk

Laura Foley is the author of seven poetry collections, including *Why I Never Finished My Dissertation*, which won an Eric Hoffer Award, and *It's This* (Salmon Press, 2021). Her poems have been read on The Writer's Almanac and appear in American Life in Poetry. She lives with her wife, Clara Gimenez, among the hills of Vermont. laurafoley.net

Patricia Fontaine teaches classes using expressive art and writing as a refuge for those living with illness, and their caregivers. Her self-published book of poems is *Lifting My Shirt: The Cancer Poems*. She lives on a big lake in northwestern Vermont with birds, wind, and a grand collection of friends and family.

Sarah Freligh is the author of *Sad Math*, winner of the

2014 Moon City Press Poetry Prize and the 2015 Whirling Prize from the University of Indianapolis; *A Brief Natural History of an American Girl* (Accents Publishing, 2012); and *Sort of Gone* (Turning Point Books, 2008). Her work has appeared in the *Cincinnati Review, SmokeLong Quarterly, Diode*, and in the anthologies *New Microfiction* and *Best Microfiction* 2019 and 2020. She received a 2009 poetry fellowship from the National Endowment for the Arts and a grant from the Constance Saltonstall Foundation in 2006.

Albert Garcia is the author of three collections of poetry: *Rainshadow* (Copper Beech Press, 1996), *Skunk Talk* (Bear Starr Press, 2005), and *A Meal Like That* (Brick Road Poetry Press, 2015). His poetry has been published in American Life in Poetry and on The Writer's Almanac, as well as in numerous journals. A former professor and dean at Sacramento Community

College, Garcia lives in Wilton, California.

Ross Gay is the author of four books of poetry: *Against Which; Bringing the Shovel Down; Catalog of Unabashed Gratitude*, winner of the 2015 National Book Critics Circle Award and the 2016 Kingsley Tufts Poetry Award; and *Be Holding* (University of Pittsburgh Press, 2020). His best-selling collection of essays, *The Book of Delights*, was released by Algonquin Books in 2019.

Crystal S. Gibbins is a Canadian American writer, the founder of *Split Rock Review*, the editor of *Rewilding: Poems for the Environment* (Flexible Press), and the author of *Now/Here* (Holy Cow! Press). Her poetry and comics have appeared in *Cincinnati Review, Coffee House Writers Project, Hayden's Ferry Review, Hobart, North American Review, Minnesota Review, Verse Daily,* The Writer's Almanac, and elsewhere. Originally from the Northwest Angle and Islands in Lake of the Woods, she now lives on Lake Superior in northern Wisconsin. crystalgibbins.com

Jessica Gigot is a poet, farmer, teacher, and musician. She is the author of *Flood Patterns* (Antrim House Books, 2015) and *Feeding Hour* (Wandering Aengus Press, 2020). Her work has appeared in *Orion, Taproot, Gastronomica, The Hopper, Mothers Always Write*, and *Poetry Northwest*. She makes artisan sheep cheese and grows organic herbs on her farm in Bow, Washington.

Alice Wolf Gilborn is the founding editor of the literary magazine *Blueline*, published by the English department at SUNY Potsdam. Her poems have appeared in *Healing the Divide* (Green Writers Press) and *After Moby-Dick* (Spinner Publications). She is the author of *Apples and Stones* (Kelsay Books, 2020); the chapbook *Taking Root* (Finishing Line Press); the nonfiction book *What Do You Do With a Kinkajou?* (Lippincott); and an essay collection, *Out of the Blue*. alicewolfgilborn.com

Nancy Miller Gomez lives in Santa Cruz, California. She cofounded Poetry in the Jails, a program that provides poetry workshops to incarcerated men and women. Her work has appeared in *New Ohio Review, The Massachusetts Review, Shenandoah, River Styx, Rattle, Verse Daily*, American Life in Poetry, and elsewhere. Her first chapbook, *Punishment*, was published by Rattle Books. She has worked as a stable hand, an attorney, and a television producer.

Amanda Gorman is the first Youth Poet Laureate of the United States. Her first poetry book is *The One for Whom Food Is Not Enough* (Penmanship Books, 2015). She is founder and executive director of One Pen One Page, which promotes literacy through free creative writing programming for underserved youth. She writes for the *New York Times*'s student newsletter, The Edit.

David Graham is the author of seven collections of poetry, including *The Honey of Earth* (Terrapin Books, 2019), *Stutter Monk* (Flume Press), and *Second Wind* (Texas Tech University Press). He coedited the anthologies *Local News: Poetry About Small Towns* (MWPH Books, 2019) and *After Confession: Poetry as Confession* (Graywolf Press, 2001). He was a faculty member at The Frost Place in Franconia, New Hampshire, where he also served as poet in residence in 1996. He taught and directed the visiting writers series at Ripon College for 28 years. He is a contributing editor and writer at Verse-Virtual, and lives in Glens Falls, New York. davidgrahampoet.com

Joy Harjo was born in Tulsa, Oklahoma, and is a member of the Mvskoke Nation. Her books of poetry include *How We Became Human: New and Selected Poems, The Woman Who Fell From the Sky*, and *She Had Some Horses*. She has received the New Mexico Governor's Award for Excellence in the Arts, a Lifetime Achievement Award from the Native Writers Circle of the Americas, and the William Carlos Williams Award from the Poetry Society of America. Harjo served as United States poet laureate from 2019–2021, and was the first Native American to serve in the position.

Jeffrey Harrison is the author of five books of poetry: *The Singing Underneath* (1988), selected by James Merrill for the National Poetry Series; *Signs of Arrival* (1996); *Feeding the Fire* (2001); *Incomplete Knowledge* (2006); and *Into Daylight* (2014), winner of Tupelo Press's Dorset Prize. A recipient of fellowships from the Guggenheim Foundation and National Endowment for the Arts, he has published poems in *The New Republic, The New Yorker, The Nation, Poetry, The Yale Review, The Hudson Review, American Poetry Review, The Paris Review, Poets of the New Century, The*

Twentieth Century in Poetry, and elsewhere. He lives in Massachusetts.

Penny Harter's poems have appeared in *Persimmon Tree, Rattle, Tiferet*, American Life in Poetry, and the anthologies *Healing the Divide* and *Poetry of Presence*. She has published 22 collections, including *A Prayer the Body Makes* (2020), *The Resonance Around Us* (2013), *One Bowl* (2012), *Recycling Starlight* (2010), and *The Night Marsh* (2008). A featured reader at the 2010 Geraldine R. Dodge Poetry Festival, she has been awarded poetry fellowships from the New Jersey State Council on the Arts; received the Mary Carolyn Davies Award from the Poetry Society of America and the William O. Douglas Nature Writing Award for her work in the anthology *American Nature Writing* 2002; and held two residencies at the Virginia Center for the Creative Arts. pennyharterpoet.com

Margaret Hasse is the author of five books of poems: *Stars*

Above, Stars Below (1985); *In a Sheep's Eye, Darling* (1993); *Milk and Tides* (2008); *Earth's Appetite* (2013); and *Between Us* (2016). She is a recipient of grants and fellowships from the National Endowment for the Arts, McKnight Foundation, Loft Literary Center's Career Initiative Program, Minnesota State Arts Board, and Jerome Foundation. Her work has been published in magazines, broadsides, and anthologies, including *Where One Voice Ends, Another Begins: 150 Years of Minnesota Poetry* and *To Sing Along the Way: Minnesota Women's Voices from Pre-Territorial Day to the Present,* and on The Writer's Almanac. She lives in Minnesota.

Jane Hirshfield's ninth and most recently published collection is *Ledger* (Knopf, 2020). A former chancellor of the Academy of American Poets, her work appears in *The New Yorker, The Atlantic, The Times Literary Supplement, The New York Review of Books,* and ten editions of *The Best American Poetry.* In 2019, she was elected into the American Academy of Arts and Sciences.

Tony Hoagland (1953–2018) was born in Fort Bragg, North Carolina. He is author of the poetry collections *Sweet Ruin* (1992), which was chosen for the Brittingham Prize in Poetry and won the Zacharis Award from Emerson College; *Donkey Gospel* (1998), winner of the James Laughlin Award; *What Narcissism Means to Me* (2003); *Rain* (2005); *Unincorporated Persons in the Late Honda Dynasty* (2010); *Application for Release from the Dream* (2015); *Recent Changes in the Vernacular* (2017); and *Priest Turned Therapist Treats Fear of God* (2018). He also published two collections of essays about poetry: *Real Sofistakashun* (2006) and *Twenty Poems That Could Save America and Other Essays* (2014).

Linda Hogan is the author of several poetry collections, including *Dark. Sweet.: New &*

Selected Poems (Coffee House Press, 2014); *Rounding the Human Corners* (2008); *The Book of Medicines* (1993), which received the Colorado Book Award; and *Seeing Through the Sun* (University of Massachusetts Press, 1985). She is writer in residence for the Chickasaw Nation and was inducted into the Chickasaw Hall of Fame. She has received fellowships from the National Endowment for the Arts and the Guggenheim Foundation, and won the Henry David Thoreau Prize for Nature Writing, a Lannan Literary Award, and a Lifetime Achievement Award from the Native Writers Circle of the Americas. She lives in Colorado.

Kathryn Hunt makes her home on the coast of the Salish Sea. Her poems have appeared in *The SUN, Rattle, Radar, Orion, Missouri Review, Frontier Poetry*, and *Narrative*. Her first collection of poems is *Long Way Through Ruin* (Blue Begonia Press). She's the recipient of residencies and awards from Ucross, Artists Trust, and Joya AIR (Spain). Her documentary film *No Place Like Home* premiered at the Venice Film Festival. Hunt is working on a memoir, *Why I Grieve I Do Not Know*. She's worked as a waitress, ship scaler, short-order cook, bookseller, printer, food bank coordinator, filmmaker, and freelance writer. kathrynhunt.net

Rob Hunter's collection of poems is *September Swim* (Spoon River Poetry Press). His poems have appeared in *Poet Lore, The Oddville Press, The Timberline Review, Sleet, Wild Violet, Straight Forward Poetry, The Blueline Anthology, Foliate Oak, Rat's Ass Review, Gray Sparrow Review*, Sheila-Na-Gig online, and others. He teaches at Burr and Burton Academy in Manchester, Vermont.

Mary Elder Jacobsen's poetry has appeared in *The Greensboro Review, Four Way Review, Green Mountains Review, storySouth, One*, and

Poetry Daily and in anthologies, including *Healing the Divide: Poems of Kindness and Connection*. Born in Washington, D.C., Jacobsen now lives in Vermont. Winner of the Lyric Memorial Prize and recipient of a Vermont Studio Center residency, she is coorganizer of Words Out Loud, an annual reading series of Vermont authors held at a still-unplugged 1823 meetinghouse.

Jacqueline Jules is the author of three chapbooks, including *Itzhak Perlman's Broken String*, winner of the 2016 Helen Kay Chapbook Prize from Evening Street Press. Her poetry has appeared in publications including *The Paterson Literary Review, Potomac Review,* and *Imitation Fruit*. She is the author of a poetry collection for young readers, *Tag Your Dreams: Poems of Play and Persistence* (Albert Whitman, 2020). She lives in Arlington, Virginia. metaphoricaltruths.blogspot .com

Garret Keizer is the author of *The World Pushes Back*, which won the 2018 X. J. Kennedy Poetry Prize, as well as eight books of prose, including *Getting Schooled* (2014), *Privacy* (2012), and *The Unwanted Sound of Everything We Want* (2010). He is a contributing editor at *Harper's* and *Virginia Quarterly Review* and a 2006 Guggenheim fellow. His poems have been published in *AGNI, The Antioch Review, Best American Poetry, Harvard Review, The Hudson Review, Ploughshares, Raritan,* and *The New Yorker*, among others. He was born in Paterson, New Jersey, and lives in Vermont with his wife.

Susan Kelly-DeWitt is a former Wallace Stegner Fellow and the author of *Gravitational Tug* (Main Street Rag, 2020), *Spider Season* (Cold River Press, 2016), *The Fortunate Islands* (Marick Press, 2008), and nine other collections. She has been a reviewer for *Library Journal*, editor in chief of the online journal Perihelion, the program director of the Sacramento Poetry Center and the Women's Wisdom Arts Program, a Poet in the Schools, a Poet in the Prisons, a blogger for Coal Hill Review, and an instructor at UC Davis. She is a member of the National Book Critics Circle and the Northern California Book Reviewers Association, and a contributing editor for Poetry Flash. She is also an exhibiting visual artist. susankelly-dewitt.com

Jane Kenyon (1947–1995) was an American poet and translator. Kenyon met the poet Donald Hall at the University of Michigan; they married in 1972 and moved to Eagle Pond Farm, Hall's ancestral home in New Hampshire. Kenyon was the poet laureate of New Hampshire when she died in April 1995 from leukemia. At the time of her death, she was working on the now-classic *Otherwise: New and Selected Poems*, which was released posthumously in 1996.

Lynne Knight is the author of six poetry collections and six chapbooks. Her work has appeared in journals, including *Poetry* and *Southern Review*. Her awards and honors include publication in *Best American Poetry*, a Prix de l'Alliance Française, a PSA Lucille Medwick Memorial Award, a Rattle Poetry Prize, and a National Endowment for the Arts grant. *I Know (Je sais)*, her translation with the author Ito Naga of his *Je sais*, appeared in 2013. She lives on Vancouver Island.

Ted Kooser, a former US poet laureate and winner of the Pulitzer Prize, has recently retired from teaching poetry in the creative writing program at the University of Nebraska in Lincoln and is now mowing grass and trying to start a weed whacker. His most recent book of poems is *Red Stilts* (Copper Canyon Press, 2020).

Danusha Laméris is the author of *The Moons of August* (Autumn House, 2014), which was chosen by Naomi Shihab Nye as winner of the Autumn House Press poetry prize. Her poems have been published in *Best American Poetry, The New York Times, American Poetry Review, Prairie Schooner, The SUN, Tin House, Gettysburg Review,* and *Ploughshares.* Her second book is *Bonfire Opera* (University of Pittsburgh Press) and she is the 2020 recipient of the Lucille Clifton Legacy Award. She is poet laureate of Santa Cruz County, California.

Heather Lanier is the author of two poetry chapbooks and the memoir *Raising a Rare Girl* (Penguin Press, 2020). Her essays and poems have appeared in *The Atlantic, The SUN, Brevity, Salon, The Southern Review, Threepenny Review,* and elsewhere. She is assistant professor of creative writing at Rowan University, and her TED talk, "Good and Bad Are Incomplete Stories We Tell Ourselves," has been viewed more than two million times.

Dorianne Laux is the author of several collections of poetry, including *What We Carry* (1994); *Smoke* (2000); *Facts*

about the Moon (2005), chosen by the poet Ai as winner of the Oregon Book Award; *The Book of Men* (2011), which was awarded the Paterson Prize; and *Only As the Day Is Long: New and Selected Poems* (2018). She has received fellowships from the Guggenheim Foundation and the National Endowment for the Arts and has been a Pushcart Prize winner. She lives with her husband, poet Joseph Millar, in North Carolina.

Li-Young Lee was born in Djakarta in 1957 to Chinese political exiles. Lee's parents came from powerful Chinese families; Lee's great grandfather was the first president of the Republic of China and Lee's father served as personal physician to Mao Zedong. Lee is the author of *The Undressing* (W. W. Norton, 2018); *Behind My Eyes* (2008); *Book of My Nights* (BOA Editions, 2001), which won the 2002 William Carlos Williams Award; *The City in Which I Love You* (1990), the 1990 Lamont Poetry Selection; and *Rose*

(1986), winner of the Delmore Schwartz Memorial Poetry Award. He lives in Chicago with his wife and sons.

Paula Gordon Lepp grew up in a tiny rural community in the Mississippi Delta. A childhood spent roaming woods and fields infuses her poems with imagery from the natural world. As an adult, her lifelong love of poetry has renewed itself, proving the axiom that it's never too late to do what you love. She now lives with her husband and two children in Charleston, West Virginia, where she is working on a collection of poetry. This is her first published work.

Annie Lighthart is a poet and teacher who started writing poetry after her first visit to an Oregon old-growth forest. She is the author of *Pax* (Salmon Poetry, 2020), *Iron String,* and *Lantern.* Her poems have been featured on The Writer's Almanac and in anthologies, including *Poetry of Presence: An Anthology of Mindfulness Poems* and *Healing the Divide.*

Her poems have also been turned into choral music, used in healing projects in Ireland, England, and New Zealand, and have traveled farther than she has.

Alison Luterman's four books of poetry are *The Largest Possible Life; See How We Almost Fly; Desire Zoo*; and *In a Time of Great Fires* (Catamaran Press, 2021). Her poems and stories have appeared in *The SUN, Rattle, Salon, Prairie Schooner, Nimrod, The Atlanta Review, Tattoo Highway*, and elsewhere. She has written an ebook of personal essays, *Feral City;* half a dozen plays; and a song cycle, *We Are Not Afraid of the Dark*; as well as two musicals, *The Chain* and *The Shyest Witch.*

Freya Manfred, a longtime Midwesterner who has lived on both coasts, is the author of two memoirs: *Frederick Manfred: A Daughter Remembers* and *Raising Twins: A True-Life Adventure.* Her nine books of poetry include *My Only Home; Swimming with a Hundred-Year-Old Snapping Turtle; Loon in Late November Water;* and *Speak, Mother.* Her poems have appeared in more than 50 anthologies. Her work celebrates the vital lifeline of nature, our fragile mortality, humor, and the passionate arc of long-term relationships. freyamanfredwriter.com

Joan Mazza worked as a microbiologist, a psychotherapist, and, before retiring, taught workshops nationally with a focus on understanding dreams and nightmares. She is the author of six books, including *Dreaming Your Real Self* (Penguin/Putnam), and her poetry has appeared in *Rattle, Valparaiso Poetry Review, Prairie Schooner, Poet Lore, The MacGuffin,* and *The Nation.* She lives in rural central Virginia, where she writes a daily poem. JoanMazza.com

Mary McCue is the author of the chapbook *Raising the Blinds* (Finishing Line Press, 2013). Her poems have appeared in *Southern Review of Poetry, Midwest Poetry Review, Streetlight Magazine, River Oak Review,* and her essays have been published in *Tampa Review, Albemarle Magazine, Chesapeake Bay,* and *Common Boundary.* A former violinist, she lives on eight acres in Albemarle County, Virginia, where deer roam and birds are safe and revered.

Michael Kiesow Moore is the author of the poetry collections *What to Pray For* and *The Song Castle* (Nodin Press). His work has appeared in *Poetry City* and *Water~Stone Review;* the anthologies *Lovejets: Queer Male Poets on 200 Years of Walt Whitman; Among the Leaves: Queer Male Poets on the Midwestern Experience;* and *A Loving Testimony: Losing Loved Ones Lost to AIDS;* and on The Writer's Almanac. He founded the Birchbark Books reading series. When he isn't drinking too much coffee, he can be found in Saint Paul, Minnesota, dancing with the Ramsey's Braggarts Morris Men.

Julie Murphy lives in Santa Cruz, California, surrounded by redwood, pine, and live oak trees. She belongs to the Community of Writers in Squaw Valley, teaches poetry at Salinas Valley State Prison, and is a founding board member of the Right to Write Press. A member of the Hive Poetry Collective, she hosts the Hive radio broadcast on KSQD. Her poems have appeared in *Massachusetts Review, CALYX, Common Ground Review, Red Wheelbarrow, Louisville Review,* and *The Alembic,* among others. She believes there is little better in life than being laid low by a good poem.

Mark Nepo is the author of the #1 *New York Times* bestseller *The Book of Awakening.* He has published 22 books and recorded 14 audio projects. Recent work includes *The Book of Soul* (St. Martin's, 2020) and *Drinking from the River of Light* (Sounds True, 2019), a Nautilus Award winner. marknepo.com and threeintentions.com

Gail Newman was born to survivors of the Polish Holocaust in a displaced persons' camp in Lansberg, Germany. She is the author of *Blood Memory,* chosen by Marge Piercy for the Marsh Hawk Press 2020 Poetry Prize, and *One World* (Moon Tide Press). She has worked as a teacher for CalPoets and as a museum educator at the Contemporary Jewish Museum in San Francisco. Her poems have appeared in *CALYX, Canary, Nimrod, Prairie Schooner,* and *Spillway*; in the anthologies *The Doll Collection* and *Ghosts of the Holocaust*; and in *America, We Call Your Name.* She is the cofounder of *Room, A Women's Literary Journal* and has edited two children's poetry collections: *C is for California* and *Dear Earth.*

Heather Newman's work has appeared in *Barrow Street, Inquisitive Eater, Matter, New Verse News, Two Hawks Quarterly, The Potomac,* and the anthology *Voices from Here.* She is a member of the South Mountain Poets and teaches at The Writers Circle in New Jersey.

Naomi Shihab Nye calls herself a "wandering poet." She has spent 40 years traveling the world to lead writing workshops and inspire students of all ages. Nye was born to a Palestinian father and an American mother and grew up in Saint Louis, Jerusalem, and San Antonio. Her books of poetry include *19 Varieties of Gazelle: Poems of the Middle East; A Maze Me: Poems for Girls; Red Suitcase; Words Under the Words; Fuel; You & Yours* (a bestseller in 2006); and *The Tiny Journalist* (BOA Editions, 2019).

January Gill O'Neil is author of *Rewilding* (2018), *Misery Islands* (2014), and *Underlife* (CavanKerry Press, 2009). She is assistant professor of English at Salem State University, and is on the board of trustees for the Association of Writers and Writing Programs and Montserrat College of Art. She served as executive director of the Massachusetts Poetry Festival from 2012 to 2018. A Cave Canem fellow, her work has appeared in the *New York Times Magazine, American Poetry Review, New England Review, Ploughshares, Ecotone*, and the Academy of American Poets Poem-a-Day series, among others. She was awarded a Massachusetts Cultural Council grant in 2018, and was named the John and Renée Grisham Writer in Residence for 2019–2020 at the University of Mississippi, Oxford. She lives with her two children in Beverly, Massachusetts.

Christen Pagett is most at home in Oregon's Willamette Valley, where she is an educator hoping to inspire teens with her love of language and all the worlds it can open. She currently spends her days pursuing an MFA in poetry at Eastern Oregon University, practicing piano, and trying new recipes on her family.

Brad Peacock is a veteran, longtime organic farmer, and former United States Senate candidate from Shaftsbury, Vermont, whose passion is to bring people closer to one another and the natural world.

Andrea Potos is the author of the poetry collections *Mothershell* (Kelsay Books), *A Stone to Carry Home* (Salmon Poetry), *Arrows of Light* (Iris Press), and *Marrow of Summer* (Kelsay Books/Aldrich Press). Her poems can be found online and in print, most recently in *Spirituality & Health, Poetry East, Cave Wall,* and *The SUN.* She received the James Hearst Poetry Prize from the *North American Review* and the William Stafford Prize from *Rosebud Magazine,* and several Outstanding Achievement Awards in Poetry from the Wisconsin Library Association. Travelling, art, cafes, and family are her greatest sources of inspiration. She lives in Madison, Wisconsin.

Laura Ann Reed grew up in the hills of Berkeley, California. She holds master's degrees in performing arts, psychology, and career counseling. She has worked as a dancer and dance instructor in the San Francisco Bay Area, and she created and worked in the role of Leadership Development Trainer for scientists and directors at the San Francisco headquarters of the US Environmental Protection Agency. She now lives with her husband in Washington State.

Jack Ridl is poet laureate of Douglas, Michigan, and the author of *Saint Peter and the Goldfinch* (Wayne State University Press); *Practicing to Walk Like a Heron,* winner of the National Gold Medal for poetry by *ForeWord Reviews/Indie Fab*; *Broken Symmetry,* the 2006 Society of Midland Authors best book of poetry; and *Losing Season* (CavanKerry Press), named best sports book of 2009 by the Institute for International Sport. The students at Hope College named him their Outstanding Professor and Favorite Professor, and the Carnegie Foundation (CASE) named him Michigan professor of the year in 1996. ridl.com

Alberto Ríos was named Arizona's first poet laureate in 2013. He is the author of many poetry collections, including *A Small Story About the Sky* (Copper Canyon, 2015), *The Dangerous Shirt* (2009), *The Theater of Night* (2006), and *The Smallest Muscle in the Human Body* (2002), which was nominated for the National Book Award.

David Romtvedt is a writer and musician from Buffalo, Wyoming. His books include *No Way: An American Tao Te Ching, Dilemmas of the Angels, Some Church, Zelestina Urza in Outer Space*, and *The Tree of Gernika. A Flower Whose Name I Do Not Know* was a selection of the National Poetry Series. A recipient of the Pushcart Prize and fellowships from the Wyoming Arts Council and the National Endowment for the Arts, Romtvedt is an avid bicyclist. With the band Ospa, he performs traditional and contemporary Basque dance music.

Katie Rubinstein is director of Seven Sisters Community Birth Center, where she has the privilege of serving women and families as a doula and apprentice midwife, and former associate director of A Network for Grateful Living. Fascinated by the many intersections of ecology, health, culture, and social change, she lives in Massachusetts with her husband, three sons, and ever-goofy canine companion, Rainer.

Marjorie Saiser's seventh collection, *Learning to Swim* (Stephen F. Austin Press, 2019), contains both poetry and memoir. Her novel-in-poems, *Losing the Ring in the River* (University of New Mexico Press) won the WILLA Award for Poetry in 2014. Saiser's poems have been published in *Rattle, Poetry East, Nimrod, Fourth River, Alaska Quarterly Review, Poet Lore, Briar Cliff Review*, *Chattahoochee Review,* and American Life in Poetry. poetmarge.com

Tracy K. Smith is author of the memoir *Ordinary Light* and four books of poetry: *Wade in the Water* (2018); *Life on Mars*, which received the 2012 Pulitzer Prize; *Duende*, recipient of the 2006 James Laughlin Award; and *The Body's Question*, which won the 2002 Cave Canem Poetry Prize. She served as the 22nd US poet laureate, 2017–2019. Smith hosts the popular podcast *The Slowdown*.

Nathan Spoon is an autistic poet whose poems have appeared in *American Poetry Review, Harvard Divinity Bulletin, Mantis, Oxford Poetry, Poetry, Reflections* (Yale Divinity School), *The Scores, South Carolina Review, Western Humanities Review*, and the anthology *What Have You Lost?*. His debut collection, *Doomsday Bunker*, and a chapbook, *My Name Is Gretchen Merryweather*, were both published in 2017. He is editor of Queerly, has been a Tennessee Williams Scholar at the Sewanee Writers' Conference, and has presented papers on

poetry and neurodiversity at the University of Pennsylvania and the Association of Literary Scholars, Critics, and Writers conference.

Kim Stafford is the founding director of the Northwest Writing Institute at Lewis & Clark College. He is the author of a dozen books of poetry and prose, including *Singer Come from Afar; The Muses Among Us: Eloquent Listening and Other Pleasures of the Writer's Craft; A Thousand Friends of Rain: New & Selected Poems; 100 Tricks Every Boy Can Do: How My Brother Disappeared; Wind on the Waves: Stories from the Oregon Coast; Having Everything Right: Essays of Place;* and *Wild Honey, Tough Salt*. He was poet laureate of Oregon, 2018–2020. He teaches and travels to raise the human spirit.

William Stafford's (1914–1993) first collection of poems, *West of Your City*, was published when he was in his mid-forties. However, by the time of his death in 1993, Stafford had published hundreds of poems. His collection *Traveling Through the Dark* won the National Book Award in 1963. Stafford also received the Award in Literature from the American Academy and Institute of Arts and Letters, a National Endowment for the Arts Senior Fellowship, and the Western States Book Award Lifetime Achievement in Poetry.

Joyce Sutphen grew up on a small farm in Stearns County, Minnesota. Her first collection of poems, *Straight Out of View*, won the Barnard New Women Poets Prize. Her recent books are *The Green House* (Salmon Poetry, 2017) and *Carrying Water to the Field: New and Selected Poems* (University of Nebraska Press, 2019). She is Minnesota poet laureate and professor emerita of literature and creative writing at Gustavus Adolphus College in Saint Peter, Minnesota.

Heather Swan is the author of *A Kinship with Ash* (Terrapin Books); the chapbook *The Edge of Damage* (Parallel Press); and the nonfiction book *Where Honeybees Thrive: Stories from the Field* (Penn State Press), which won the Sigurd F. Olson Nature Writing Award. Her poems have appeared in *Poet Lore, Cold Mountain, Phoebe, Iris, Midwestern Gothic, The Hopper,* and *Basalt*. Her nonfiction has appeared in *Aeon, Minding Nature, ISLE, Belt Magazine,* and *Edge Effects*. She teaches environmental literature and writing at University of Wisconsin–Madison.

Wally Swist's books include *Huang Po and the Dimensions of Love* (Southern Illinois University Press, 2012); *The Daodejing: A New Interpretation* (Lamar University Literary Press, 2015); and *Invocation* (2015). His poems have appeared in *Appalachia, Commonweal, Miramar, North American Review, Rattle, Sunken Garden Poetry, upstreet,* and on The Writer's Almanac. Swist lives in South Amherst, Massachusetts.

Tess Taylor is the author of *Rift Zone* (Red Hen Press); *The Forage House*; *Work & Days*, named one of the best books of poetry in 2016 by the *New York Times*; and *The Misremembered World*, selected by Eavan Boland for the Poetry Society of America's inaugural chapbook fellowship. She published *Last West* (2020) as part of the exhibition *Dorothea Lange: Words & Pictures* at the Museum of Modern Art in New York. She is a poetry reviewer for NPR's All Things Considered.

Francine Marie Tolf is the author of *Rain, Lilies, Luck* (North Star Press, 2010) as well as a memoir, essay collection, and a number of chapbooks. Her poems and essays have been published in numerous journals. She lives and works in Minneapolis.

Angela Narciso Torres is the author of *Blood Orange*, winner of the Willow Books Literature Award for Poetry; *To the Bone* (Sundress, 2020); and *What Happens Is Neither* (Four Way Books, 2021). Her work has appeared in *Poetry, Missouri Review, Quarterly West, Cortland Review,* and *PANK*. Torres received the 2019 Yeats Poetry Prize (W. B. Yeats Society of New York), and has received fellowships from the Bread Loaf Writers' Conference, Illinois Arts Council, and Ragdale Foundation. Born in Brooklyn and raised in Manila, she is an editor for *RHINO Poetry*.

Rosemerry Wahtola Trommer lives on the banks of the San Miguel River in southwest Colorado. She served as Colorado Western Slope poet laureate (2015–2017) and San Miguel County poet laureate (2007–2011). She cohosts *Emerging Form* (a podcast on creative process), is cofounder of Secret Agents of Change, and codirects Telluride's Talking Gourds Poetry Club. Her poetry has appeared in *O Magazine* and *Rattle*, on A Prairie Home Companion, and on river rocks. She has written 13 poetry collections, most recently *Hush*, winner of the Halcyon Prize for poems of human ecology. She teaches poetry for addiction recovery programs, hospice, mindfulness retreats, women's retreats, scientists, and others. ahundredfallingveils.com and wordwoman.com

Ron Wallace is the author of more than 20 books and chapbooks of poetry, fiction, and criticism, including *For Dear Life, For a Limited Time Only*, and *Long for This World: New and Selected Poems*. Founder and director of the University of Wisconsin–Madison's program in creative writing, he is Felix Pollak Professor Emeritus and editor of the University of Wisconsin Press Poetry Series. He divides his time between Madison and a 40-acre farm in Bear Valley, Wisconsin, where he tends a large vegetable garden, helps his wife, Peg, restore prairie, bird-watches, and mows eight miles of grass and sweet clover with his power push mower.

Connie Wanek was born in Wisconsin, raised in New Mexico, and now lives in Duluth, Minnesota. Her first book, *Bonfire* (New Rivers, 1997), won the New Voices Award. She is also the author of *Hartley Field* (Holy Cow!, 2002), *On Speaking Terms* (Copper Canyon, 2010), *Rival Gardens: New and Selected Poems* (University of Nebraska Press, 2016), and the chapbook *Consider the Lilies: Mrs. God Poems* (Will o' the Wisp, 2018). Forthcoming from Candlewick Press is a children's book of poetry cowritten with Ted Kooser.

Laura Grace Weldon is the author of *Blackbird* (Grayson Books, 2019) and *Tending* (Aldrich Press, 2013), as well as a handbook for alternative education, *Free Range Learning* (Hohm Press, 2010). She was named 2019 Ohio Poet of the Year. Her background includes teaching nonviolence classes, facilitating support groups for abuse survivors, and writing collaborative poetry with nursing home residents. lauragraceweldon.com

Cynthia White's poems have appeared in *Massachusetts Review, Narrative, ZYZZYVA, Grist,* and *Catamaran,* among others. She won the Julia Darling Memorial Prize from Kallisto Gaia Press. She lives in Santa Cruz, California.

Diana Whitney writes across genres on feminism, motherhood, and sexuality. Her first book, *Wanting It,* won the Rubery Book Award in poetry. She was the poetry critic for the *San Francisco Chronicle,* where she featured women authors and LGBTQ voices in her column. Her writing has appeared in the *New York Times, Glamour,* the *Washington Post, Kenyon Review,* and elsewhere. A feminist activist, she is a senior contributing editor at HealthyWomen.org. Her latest project is *How to Be Real: Poems for Girls Becoming Themselves* (Workman, 2021). diana-whitney.com

Michelle Wiegers is a poet and life coach based in Southern Vermont. Her work has appeared in *Healing the Divide: Poems of Kindness and Connection, Birchsong Anthology,* and *Third Wednesday,* among other journals. In her mind-body life coaching work, she is a passionate advocate for those in chronic pain.
michellewiegers.com

Katherine Williams's poems have been published in *Poet Lore, The Northern Virginia Review, Voices,* and the anthologies *The Widows' Handbook* and *The Poet's Cookbook.* She is associate professor emerita at George Washington University and works as a psychologist and art therapist in private practice.

CREDITS

TRANSFORM YOUR LIFE
WITH MORE BOOKS FROM STOREY

Wake Up Grateful by Kristi Nelson

Learn to see the abundance and opportunity in every moment. With daily exercises and prompts for deep reflection, this book offers profound personal change through the practice of taking nothing for granted.

Everyday Gratitude by A Network for Grateful Living

Invite joy with this beautiful hand-lettered collection of uplifting quotes from Maya Angelou, Confucius, Anne Frank, and dozens of other thoughtful writers. Reflections and practices help you consciously appreciate life's abundance, every day.

Forest Bathing Retreat by Hannah Fries

This inspiring volume of stunning nature photography, evocative text, and mindfulness exercises is your guide to the healing peace and restorative power of trees and nature.

*From Our Sister Company, **Algonquin Books***

The Book of Delights by Ross Gay

This spirited collection of short lyric essays, written daily over a tumultuous year, reminds us of the pleasure of celebrating ordinary wonders.

Join the conversation. Share your experience with this book, learn more about Storey Publishing's authors, and read original essays and book excerpts at storey.com.
Look for our books wherever quality books are sold or call 800-441-5700.